Laura Preston

A Boy's Trip Across the Plains

Laura Preston

A Boy's Trip Across the Plains

ISBN/EAN: 9783744686051

Printed in Europe, USA, Canada, Australia, Japan

Cover: Foto ©Andreas Hilbeck / pixelio.de

More available books at **www.hansebooks.com**

A BOY'S TRIP

ACROSS THE PLAINS.

By LAURA PRESTON,

AUTHOR OF "YOUTH'S HISTORY OF CALIFORNIA."

NEW YORK:
A. ROMAN & COMPANY, PUBLISHERS.
SAN FRANCISCO:
417 AND 419 MONTGOMERY STREET.
1868.

Entered according to Act of Congress in the year 1868,
By A. ROMAN & COMPANY,
In the Clerk's Office of the District Court of the United States
For the Southern District of New York.

TO

LOUIS AND MARY,

THE ELDEST

OF A BEVY OF NEPHEWS AND NIECES,

THIS LITTLE WORK

IS AFFECTIONATELY DEDICATED,

WITH THE HOPE

THAT AS IT HAS ALREADY RECEIVED THEIR FAVORABLE CRITICISM,

IT MAY MEET THAT OF ALL YOUTHFUL LOVERS

OF ADVENTURE.

San Francisco, June, 1868.

A BOY'S TRIP
ACROSS THE PLAINS.

BY LAURA PRESTON.

CHAPTER I.

In the village of W——, in western Missouri, lived Mrs. Loring and her son Guy, a little boy about ten years old. They were very poor, for though Mr. Loring, during his life time was considered rich, and his wife and child had always lived comfortably, after his death, which occurred when Guy was about eight years old, they found that there were so many people to whom Mr. Loring owed money, that when the debts were paid there was but little left for the widow and her only child. That would not have been so bad had they had friends able or willing to assist them, but Mrs. Loring found that most of her friends had gone with her wealth, which, I am sorry to say, is apt to be the case the world over.

As I have said, when Mrs. Loring became a widow she was both poor and friendless, she was also very delicate. She had never worked in her life, and although she attempted to do so, in order to support herself and little Guy, she found it almost impossible to earn enough to supply them with food. She opened a little school, but could get only a few scholars, and they paid her so little that she was obliged also to take in sewing. This displeased the parents of her pupils and they took away their children, saying "she could not do two things at once."

This happened early in winter when they needed money far more than at any other season. But though Mrs. Loring sewed a great deal during that long, dreary winter, she was paid so little that both young Guy and herself often felt the pangs of cold and hunger. Perhaps they need not have done so, if Mrs. Loring had told the village people plainly that she was suffering, for I am sure they would have given her food. But she was far too proud to beg or to allow her son to do so. She had no objection that he should work, for toil is honorable—but in the winter there was little a boy of ten could do, and although Guy was very industrious it was not often he could obtain employment. So they every day grew poorer, for although they had no money their clothing and scanty furniture did not know it, and wore out much quicker than that of rich people seems to do.

Yet through all the trials of the long winter Mrs. Loring did not despair; she had faith to believe that God was bringing her sorrows upon her for the best, and would remove them in his own good time. This, she would often say to Guy when she saw him look sad, and he would glance up brightly with the reply, "I am sure it is for the best, mother. You have always been so good I am sure God will not let you suffer long. I think we shall do very well when the Spring comes. We shall not need a fire then, or suffer for the want of warm clothing and I shall be able to go out in the fields to work, and shall earn so much money that you will not have to sew so much, and get that horrid pain in your chest."

But when the Spring came Guy did not

find it so easy to get work as he had fancied it would be, for there were a great many strong, rough boys that would do twice as much work in the day as one who had never been used to work, and the farmers would employ them, of course. So poor Guy grew almost disheartened, and his mother with privation and anxiety, fell very sick.

Although afraid she would die she would not allow Guy to call any of the village people in, for she felt that they had treated her very unkindly and could not bear that they should see how very poor she was. She however told Guy he could go for a doctor, and he did so, calling in one that he had heard often visited the poor and charged them nothing.

This good man whose name was Langley, went to Mrs. Loring's, and soon saw both how indigent and how ill the poor woman was. He was very kind and gave her medicines and such food as she could take, although it hurt her pride most bitterly to accept them. He also gave Guy some work to do, and he was beginning to hope that his mother was getting well, and that better days were coming, when going home one evening from his work he found his mother crying most bitterly. He was in great distress at this, and begged her to tell him what had happened. At first she refused to do so, but at last said :—

"Perhaps, Guy, it is best for me to tell you all, for if trouble must come, it is best to be prepared for it. Sit here on the bed beside me, and I will try to tell you:"

She then told him that Doctor Langley had been there that afternoon, and had told her very gently, but firmly, that she was in a consumption and would die.

"Unless," she added, "I could leave this part of the country. With an entire change of food and air, he told me that I might live many years. But you know, my dear boy, it is impossible for me to have that, so I must make up my mind to die. That would not be so hard to do if it were not for leaving you alone in this uncharitable world."

Poor Mrs. Loring who had been vainly striving to suppress her emotions, burst into tears, and Guy who was dreadfully shocked and alarmed, cried with her. It seemed so dreadful to him that his mother should die when a change of air and freedom from anxiety might save her. He thought of it very sadly for many days, but could see no way of saving his mother. He watched her very closely, and although she seemed to gain a little strength as the days grew warmer, and even sat up, and tried to sew, he was not deceived into thinking she would get well, for the doctor had told him she never would, though for the summer she might appear quite strong.

He was walking slowly and sadly through the street one day, thinking of this, when he heard two gentlemen who were walking before him, speak of California.

"Is it true," said one, "that Harwood is going there?"

"Yes," said the other, "he thinks he can better his condition by doing so."

"Do you know what steamer he will leave on?" asked the first speaker.

"He is not going by steamer," replied the second, "as Aggie is quite delicate, he has decided to go across the plains."

"Ah! indeed. When do they start?"

"As soon as possible. Mrs. Harwood

told me to-day, that the chief thing they were waiting for, was a servant. Aggie needs so much of her care that she must have a nurse for the baby, and she says it seems impossible to induce a suitable person to go. Of course she doesn't want a coarse, uneducated servant, but some one she can trust, and who will also be a companion for herself during the long journey."

The gentlemen passed on, and Guy heard no more, but he stood quite still in the street, and with a throbbing heart, thought, "Oh! if my mother could go across the plains, it would cure her. Oh! if Mrs. Harwood would but take her as a nurse. I know she is weak, but she could take care of a little baby on the plains much better than she can bend over that hard sewing here, and besides I could help her. Oh! if Mrs. Harwood would only take her. I'll find out where she lives, and ask her to do so."

He had gained the desired information and was on his way to Mrs. Harwood's house before he remembered that his mother might not consent to go if Mrs. Harwood was willing to take her. He knew she was very proud, and had been a rich lady herself once, and would probably shrink in horror from becoming a servant. His own pride for a moment revolted against it, but his good sense came to his aid, and told him it was better to be a servant than die. He went on a little farther, and then questioned himself whether it would not be better to go first and tell his mother about it, and ask her consent to speak to Mrs. Harwood. But it was a long way back, and as he greatly feared his mother would not allow him to come, and would probably be much hurt at his suggesting such a thing, he determined to act for once without her knowledge, and without further reflection walked boldly up to Mrs. Harwood's door. It was open, and when he knocked some one called to him to come in.

He did so, although for a moment he felt inclined to run away. There was a lady in the room, and four children—two large boys, a delicate looking girl about five years old, and a baby boy who was sitting on the floor playing with a kitten, but who stopped and stared at Guy as he entered.

The other children did the same, and Guy was beginning to feel very timid and uncomfortable, when the lady asked who he wished to see.

He told her Mrs. Harwood, and the eldest boy said, "That's ma's name, isn't it, ma? What do you want of ma? say!"

Guy said nothing to the rude boy, but told Mrs. Harwood what he had heard on the street.

"It is true," she said kindly, "I do want a nurse. Has some one sent you here to apply for the place?"

"No, ma'am," he replied, "no one sent me, but—but—I came—of myself—because—I thought—my—mother—might—perhaps suit you."

"Why, that is a strange thing for a little boy to do!" exclaimed Mrs. Harwood.

"Hullo, Gus," cried the boy that had before spoken, "here's a friend of mine; guess he's the original Young America, 'stead of me!"

"George, be silent," said his mother, very sternly. "Now, child," she continued, turning again to Guy, "you may tell me how you ever thought of doing so strange a thing as applying for a place for your mother, unless she told you to do so. Is she unkind to you? Do you want her to leave you?"

"Oh, no, she is very, very kind," said Guy, earnestly, "and I wouldn't be parted from her for the world." He then forgot all his fears, and eagerly told the lady how sick his mother had been, and how sure he was that the trip across the plains would cure her, and, above all, told how good and kind she was; "she nursed me," he concluded, very earnestly, "and you see what a big boy I am!"

Mrs. Harwood smiled so kindly that he was almost certain she would take his mother; but his heart fell, when she said: "I am very sorry that your mother is sick, but I don't think I can take her with me; and besides, Mr. Harwood would not like to have another boy to take care of."

"But I will take care of myself," cried

Guy, "and help a great deal about the wagons. Oh, ma'am, if you would only take me, I would light the fires when you stopped to camp, and get water, and do a great many things, and my mother would do a great deal too."

Mrs. Harwood shook her head, and poor Guy felt so downcast that he was greatly inclined to cry. The boys laughed, but the little girl looked very sorry, and said to him:

"Don't look so sad; perhaps mamma will yet take your mother, and I will take you. I want you to go. You look good and kind, and wouldn't let George tease me."

"That I wouldn't," said Guy, looking pityingly upon the frail little creature, and wondering how any one could think of being unkind to her.

"What is your name?" asked the little one.

"Guy," he replied, and the boys burst into a laugh.

"Oh, let us take him with us, ma," cried George, "it would be such capital fun to have a 'guy' with us all the time, to make us laugh. Oh, ma, do let him go."

"Yes, mamma, do let him go," said little Aggie, taking her brother's petition quite in earnest. "I am sure he could tell me lots of pretty stories, and you wouldn't have to tell me 'Bluebeard' and 'Cinderella,' until you were tired of telling, and I of hearing them."

Now Mrs. Harwood was very fond of her children, and always liked to indulge them, if she possibly could, especially her little, delicate Agnes. She thought to herself, as she saw them together, that he might, in reality, be very useful during the trip, especially as Agnes had taken so great a fancy to him; so she decided, instead of sending him away, as she had first intended, to keep him a short time, and if he proved as good a boy as he appeared, to go with him to his mother and see what she could do for her. Accordingly, she told Guy to stay with the children for an hour, while she thought of the matter. He did so, and as she watched him closely, she saw, with surprise, that he amused Agnes by his lively stories, the baby by his antics, and was successful not only in preventing Gus and George from quarreling, but in keeping friendly with them himself.

"This boy is very amiable and intelligent," she said to herself, "and as he loves her so well, it is likely his mother has the same good qualities. I will go around to see her, and if she is well enough to travel, and is the sort of person I imagine,

I will certainly try to take her with me."

She sent Guy home with a promise to that effect, and in great delight he rushed into the house, and told his mother what he had done. At first she was quite angry, and Guy felt very wretchedly over his impulsive conduct; but when he told her how kind the lady was, and how light her duties would probably be, she felt almost as anxious as Guy himself, that Mrs. Harwood should find her strong and agreeable enough to take the place.

Mr. and Mrs. Harwood came the next day, and were much pleased with Mrs. Loring, and perhaps more so with Guy, though they did not say so. The doctor came in while they were there, and was delighted with the project, assuring Mrs. Loring that the trip would greatly benefit her, and privately telling Mr. and Mrs.

Harwood what a good woman she was, and how willing she was to do any thing honorable for the support of herself and her little boy. So they decided to take her.

"We will give you ten dollars a month," said they, "so you will not be quite penniless when you get to California."

Mrs. Loring thanked them most heartily, and Guy felt as if all the riches of the world had been showered down upon them.

"You look like an energetic little fellow," said Mr. Harwood to Guy, as they were going away, "and I hope you will continue to be one, else I shall leave you on the plains. Remember, I'll have no laggards in my train."

Guy promised most earnestly to be as alert and industrious as could be desired, and full of good intentions and delightful hopes, went back to his mother to talk of what might happen during their TRIP ACROSS THE PLAINS.

CHAPTER II.

How quickly the next two weeks of Guy Loring's life flew by. He was busy and therefore had no time to notice how often his mother sighed deeply when he talked of the free, joyous life they should lead on the plains. There seemed to her little prospect of freedom or pleasure in becoming a servant; yet she said but little about it to Guy as she did not wish to dampen the ardor of his feelings, fearing that the stern reality of an emigrant's life would soon throw a cloud over his blissful hopes. Even Guy himself sometimes felt half inclined to repent his impulsiveness, for George Harwood constantly reminded him of it by calling him " Young America " and asking him if he had no other servants to hire out.

Guy bore all these taunts very quietly, and even laughed at them, and made himself so useful and agreeable to every one, that on the morning of the start from W——, Mr. Harwood was heard to say he would as soon be without one of his best men as little Guy Loring.

It was a beautiful morning in May, 1855, upon which Mr. Harwood's train left W——. Guy was amazed at the number of people, of horses and wagons, and at the preparations that had been made for the journey. Besides Mr. Harwood's family there was that of his cousin, Mr. Frazer; five young men from St. Louis, and another with his two sisters from W——. Guy could not but wonder that so many people should travel together, for he thought it would have been much pleasanter for each family to be alone, until he heard that there were a great many Indians upon the plains who often robbed, and sometimes murdered small parties of travelers.

As the long train of wagons and cattle moved along the narrow streets of the quiet village, Guy thought of all he had read of the caravans that used to cross the desert sands of Arabia. "Doesn't it remind you of them?" he said, after mentioning his thoughts to George Harwood who was standing near.

"Not a bit" he replied with a laugh. "Those great, strong, covered wagons don't look much like the queer old caravans did I guess, and neither the mules or oxen are like camels, besides the drivers haven't any turbans on their heads, and the people altogether look much more like Christians than Arabs."

Guy was quite abashed, and not daring

to make any other comparisons, asked Gus to tell him the name of the owner of each wagon as it passed.

"The first was father's," he answered readily, "the next two cousin James Frazer's. The next one belongs to William Graham, and his two sisters, the next two to the young men from St. Louis, and the other six are baggage wagons."

Guy could ask nothing more as Mr. Harwood called to him to help them in driving some unruly oxen that were in the rear of the train. Next he was ordered to run back to the village for some article that had been forgotten, next to carry water to the teamsters, then to run with messages from one person to another until he was so tired, he thoroughly envied George and Gus their comfortable seats in one of the baggage wagons, and was delighted at last to hear the signal to halt.

Although they had been traveling all day they were but a few miles from the village, and the people in spite of the wearisome labors of the day scarcely realized that they had begun a long and perilous journey. To most of them it seemed like a picnic party, but to poor little Guy, it seemed a very tiresome one as he assisted in taking a small cooking-stove from Mr. Harwood's baggage wagon. As soon as it was set up, in the open air, at a short distance from the wagons, he was ordered to make a fire. There was a quantity of dry wood at hand, and soon he had the satisfaction of seeing a cheerful blaze. Asking Gus to take care that it did not go out, he took a kettle from the wagon and went to the spring for water.

Every person was too busy to notice whether Gus watched the fire or not. Some were building fires for themselves, some unhitching the horses from the traces, unyoking the oxen, and giving them water and feed. Guy thought he had never beheld so busy a scene as he came back with the water, hoping that his fire was burning brightly. Alas! not a spark was to be seen, Gus had gone with George to see the cows milked, and poor Guy had to build the fire over again. Although he was very tired he would have gone to work cheerfully enough, had not Mrs. Harwood, who was wishing to warm some milk for the baby reprimanded him severely for his negligence. He thought the fire would never burn, and was almost ready to cry with vexation and fatigue. Indeed two great tears did gather in his eyes, and roll slowly over his cheeks. He tried to wipe them away, but was not quick enough to prevent George Harwood who had returned from milking, from seeing them.

"Hullo!" he cried, catching Guy by the ears and holding back his head that everybody might see his face, "here is 'Young America' boo-hoo-ing, making a reg'lar 'guy' of himself sure enough. Has somebody stepped on his poor 'ittle toe?" he added with mock tenderness, as if he was talking to a little child; "never mind, hold up your head, or you'll put the fire out with your tears; just see how they make it fizzle: why, how salt they must be!"

Guy had the good sense neither to get angry, or to cry, at this raillery, although he found it hard to abstain from doing both. But he remembered in time that his mother had told him the only way to silence George was to take no notice of him.

"Guy," said Mrs. Harwood, who had just come from the wagon, with some meat to be cooked for supper, "I want you to go to your mother, and amuse Aggie."

He went joyfully as he had not seen his mother since morning. He uttered an exclamation of surprise when he entered the wagon in which she was seated, it was so different from what he had imagined it. It was covered with thick oil-cloth, which was quite impervious to rain; on the floor was a carpet, over head a curious sort of rack that held all manner of useful things, guns, fishing poles and lines, game bags, baskets of fruit, sewing materials, books, and even glass-ware and crockery. Guy thought he had never seen so many things packed in so small a space. There were at the rear of the wagon and along the sides, divans, or cushioned benches, made of pine boxes covered with cloth and padded, so that they made very comfortable seats or beds. As Guy saw no sheets or blankets upon the divans, he was at a loss to know how the sleepers would keep warm, until his mother raised the cushioned lid of one of the boxes, and showed him a quantity of coverlets and blankets, packed tightly therein.

There was a large, round lamp suspended from the center of the wagon, and as Guy looked at his mother's cheerful surroundings he could not but wonder that she sighed when he spoke of the dark, lonesome lodgings they had left, until he suddenly remembered that she had been nursing the heavy, fretful baby, and trying to amuse Aggie all the day.

Poor little Aggie was looking very sad, and often said she was very tired of the dull wagon, and was cold, too. Guy told her of the bright camp-fires that were burning beside the wagons, and asked her to go out with him to see them, for although he was very tired and would gladly have rested in the wagon, he was willing to weary himself much more if he could do anything to please the sickly little girl.

"Oh I should like to go very much," cried Aggie eagerly, "Go and ask ma if I can! It will be such fun to see the fires burning and all the people standing around them."

Mrs. Harwood was willing for Guy to take Aggie out, if he would be careful of her, and so he went back and told the anxious little girl.

"Ah! but I am afraid you won't take care of me," she exclaimed hastily. "Nobody but mamma takes care of me. George and Gus always lets me fall, and then I cry because I am hurt, and then papa whips them, and I cry harder than ever because *they* are hurt."

"But we will have no hurting or crying this time," replied Guy as he helped Aggie out of the wagon, thinking what a tender-hearted girl she must be to cry to see George Harwood whipped, he was sure that he should not, "for," said Guy to himself, "we should never cry over what we think will do people good."

How busy all the people seemed to be as Guy, with Aggie by his side walked among them. Both were greatly pleased at the novel scene presented to their view. Two cooking stoves were sending up from their black pipes thick spirals of smoke, while half a dozen clouds of the same arose from as many fires, around which were gathered men and women busily engaged in preparing the evening meal. Tea and coffee were steaming, beefsteaks broiling, slices of bacon sputtering in the frying pans, each and every article sending forth most appetizing odors.

Aggie was anxious to see how her

father's baggage wagons were arranged and where they stood. They proved to be the very best of the train, but they were so interested in all they saw and heard that they did not appear long in reaching them.

"What a nice time we shall have on the Plains," exclaimed Aggie. "I shall want you to take me out among the wagons every night. I never thought such great, lumbering things could look so pretty. I thought the cloth coverings so coarse and yellow this morning, and now by the blaze of the fires they appear like banks of snow."

So she talked on until Guy had led her past the fires, the groups were busy and cheerful people, the lowing cattle and the tired horses and mules which were quietly munching their fodder and corn, until they reached the baggage wagons. In one of them they found a lamp burning, and by its light they saw how closely it was packed. There were barrels of beef, pork, sugar, flour, and many other articles which were requisite for a long journey. There were boxes too, of tea, coffee, rice, crackers and many other edibles, and in one corner, quite apart from these a number of flasks of powder. There were also several guns, some spades and other tools, and a great many things which Guy and Aggie thought useless, but proved very valuable at a later time.

"I wonder what papa brought so many guns for?" said little Aggie. "And all the others have them too. I should think they would be afraid to sleep in a wagon with so many guns and so much powder in it."

"Men should not be afraid of anything," said Guy very bravely, "and at any rate not of guns and powder, for with them they can guard their lives and property from the Indians."

"The Indians!" cried Aggie opening her eyes very wide with fright and surprise. "Are there Indians on the Plains?"

"Yes. But don't be frightened," replied Guy. "They shall not harm you, and perhaps we may not see any."

"Oh, I hope we shan't. Let us go back to mother, it is getting dark, and I'm so frightened. Oh, dear! Oh, dear!"

Aggie's alarm rather amused Guy, but he soothed her very kindly and told her he would take her to her mother, and they had just left the wagon, when a terrible figure, wrapped in a buffalo robe, and brandishing in his hand a small hatchet, jumped with an awful yell into the path before them.

Poor Aggie caught Guy's arm and screaming with terror begged him to save her from the Indian. For a moment Guy himself was startled, then as the monster came nearer he jumped forward, wrested the hatchet from its grasp, and with hands neither slow nor gentle, tore the buffalo robe aside and administered some hearty cuffs to the crest-fallen George Harwood.

"Let me go," he said piteously. "Don't you see who I am? I'll tell my father, so I will."

"You are a fine Indian," said Guy, contemptuously, "just able to frighten little girls."

"I can whip you," exclaimed George, as he saw Guy was preparing to lead Aggie to her mother. "Just come on!"

"No," said Guy, who had already proved the cowardice of his opponent, "I am quite willing always to protect my master's daughter from Indians, but not to fight his sons."

"Bravely spoken my little man," exclaimed Mr. Harwood, who had approached them unperceived.

"He's a coward," whimpered George, "he struck me!"

"I saw all that passed," replied Mr. Harwood, "and I wonder that he acted so well. I shall make him from henceforth Aggie's especial defender, and he can strike whoever molests her, whether it be an Indian or any one else."

George walked sullenly away, and Mr. Harwood, Aggie and Guy turned toward the camp-fires, and passing three or four, reached that of their own party. At some little distance from it was spread a table-cloth covered with plates, dishes of bread, vegetables and meat, cups of steaming coffee, and other articles. On the grass around this lowly table the family were seated, all cheerful and all by the labors of the day blessed with an appetite that rendered their first meal in camp perfectly delicious.

But for Guy, a dreary hour followed the supper, there were dishes to wash, water to fetch, and fires to pile high with wood. Guy almost envied his mother the task of rocking the baby to sleep, yet was glad that he was able to do the harder work which would otherwise have fallen on her hands.

It was quite late when all his work was done, and he was able to sit for a few moments by the camp-fire. He had just begun to tell Aggie of "Jack, the Giant Killer's" wonderful exploits, when Mr. Harwood rang a large bell, and all the people left their fires and congregated about his. Mr. Harwood then stood up with a book in his hand and told them in a few words what a long and perilous journey they had undertaken, and asked them to join with him in entreating God's blessing upon them. He then read a short chapter from the bible and all knelt down while he offered up a prayer for guidance and protection.

Aggie whispered to Guy, as she bade him "good-night," that after that prayer she should not be afraid of the Indians, and went very contentedly to her mother's wagon, while Guy followed Gus and George to the one in which they were to sleep.

They were all too weary to talk, and wrapping their blankets around them lay down, and Gus and George were soon fast asleep. Guy lay awake some time, looking out at the bright fires—the sleeping cattle, the long row of wagons, seeing in fancy far beyond the wide expanse of prairies, the snowy peaks of the Rocky Mountains, and at last in his peaceful sleep, the golden land of California.

CHAPTER III.

It seemed to Guy but a few short moments before he was aroused from sleep by the voice of Mr. Harwood, calling to him to light the fire in the stove.

He started up, for a moment, thinking himself in the poor lodging at W——, and wondering why his mother had called him so early. But the sight of the closely packed wagon, and his sleeping companions, immediately recalled to his remembrance his new position and its many duties. He hurriedly left the wagon, but as it was still quite dark to his sleepy eyes, he had to wait a few moments and look cautiously around, before he could decide which way to turn his steps.

The first objects he saw, were the camp-fires, which were smouldering slowly away as if the gray dawn that was peeping over the hills was putting them to shame. He thought to himself "I am the first up," but on going forward a few steps, found himself mistaken, several of the men were moving briskly about, rousing the lazy horses and oxen, or building fires.

"I shall have to be quick," thought Guy, "or I shall be the last instead of the first!" and he went to work with such ardor that he had a fire in the stove, and the kettle boiling over it before any one came to cook breakfast.

He was glad to see that his mother was the first to leave Mr. Harwood's wagon, for he wanted to have a chat with her alone, but his pleasure was soon turned to sorrow when he saw how weary she looked. He feared, at first, that she was ill, but she told him that the baby had passed a restless night and kept her awake. Poor Mrs. Loring could not take up her new life as readily as Guy, and even while she encouraged him always to look upon the bright side, she very often saw only the dark herself.

But no one could long remain dull or unhappy that beautiful spring morning. The dawn grew brighter as the fires died away, and at last the sun extinguished them altogether by the glory of his presence, as he rose above the distant hills.

Guy thought he had never beheld so lovely a scene. There was the busy, noisy camp before him, and beyond it the calm beauty of freshly budding forests, standing forth in bold relief from the blue sky which bore on its bosom the golden sphere whence emanate all light and heat, God's gifts that make our earth so lovely and so fruitful.

Those were Guy's thoughts as he moved about, willingly assisting his mother, and the two young girls who, with their brother had left W—— to seek their fortunes in the far West. Guy pitied them very much for they were unused to work and had at that time a great deal to do. So when he went to the spring for water, he brought also a pailful for them, and when he had a leisure moment, he did any little chores for them that he could. He had not noticed them much the night before, but that morning he became quite well acquainted with them; discovered that the elder was called Amy, and the younger Carrie, and that they were both very pleasant, and apreciative of all little acts of kindness.

Before the sun was an hour high, the breakfast had been partaked of, the camp furniture replaced in the wagons and the train put in motion.

Slowly and steadily the well-trained mules and the patient oxen wended their way towards the Missouri River, and so for nearly two weeks the march was kept up with no incident occurring to break its monotony, save the daily excitement of breaking camp at noon and after a tiresome walk of a dozen miles or more, building the watch fires at night, and talking over the events of the day.

I think had it not been for Aggie, Guy would often have fallen to sleep as soon as he joined the circle round the fire, for he was generally greatly wearied by the labors of the day. Every one found something for Guy to do, and as he never shirked his work as many boys do, he found but little time for rest, and none for play.

So, as I have said, he was usually so tired at night that he would certainly have fallen asleep as soon as he gained a quiet nook by the fire, but for little Aggie, who never failed to take a seat close beside him and ask for a story. So with the little girl on side, Gus on the other, and George seated where he could hear without appearing to listen, Guy would tell them all the wonderful tales he had ever read, and many beside that were never printed or even known before.

Those hours spent around the glowing fires, were happy ones to the children. Even George, when he looked up at the countless stars looking down upon them from the vast expanse of heaven, was quieted and seldom annoyed either Guy or his eager listeners by his ill-timed jests or practical jokes.

"I wish," said little Aggie one evening, when she was sitting by the fire with her curly head resting on Guy's arms, "that you would tell me where all the pretty sparks go when they fly upward."

"Why, they die and fall to the earth again," exclaimed George, laughing.

"I dont think they do," replied Aggie, "I think the fire-flies catch them and carry them away under their wings."

"And hang them for lamps in butterflies' houses," suggested Guy.

"Oh yes," cried Aggie, clapping her hand in delight. "Do tell us about them, Guy! I am sure you can!"

So Guy told her about the wonderful bowers in the centre of large roses where the butterflies rest at night, of the great parlor in the middle of all, whose walls are of the palest rose and whose ceiling is upheld by pillars of gold, and of the bed chambers on either hand with their crimson hangings and their atmosphere of odors so sweet that the very butterflies sometimes become intoxicated with its deliciousness, and sleep until the rude sun opens their chamber doors and dries the dew-drops upon their wings. And he told them too, how the butterflies gave a ball one night. All the rose parlors were opened and at each door two fire-flies stood, each with a glowing spark of flame to light the gay revellers to the feast.

For a long time they patiently stood watching the dancers, and recounting to each other the origin of the tiny lamps they held.

"I," said one, "caught the last gleam from a widow's hearth, and left her and her children to freeze; but I couldn't help that for my Lady Golden Wing told me to bring the brightest light to-night."

"Yet you are scarcely seen," replied his companion, " and 'tis right your flame should be dull, for the cruelty you showed toward the poor widow, I caught my light from a rich man's fire and injured no one, and that is how my lamp burns brighter than yours."

"At any rate I have the comfort of knowing mine is as bright as that of some others here."

"Nay even mine is brighter than yours," cried a fly from a neighboring rose. " I would scorn to get my light as you did yours. I caught mine from the tip of a match with which a little servant-maid was lighting a fire for her sick mistress. It was the last match in the house too, and it made me laugh till I ached to hear how mistress and maid groaned over my fun."

" You cannot say much of my cruelty when you think of your own," commented the first, " nor need you wonder that your lamp is dull. But look at the light at my Lord Spangle Down's door, it is the most glorious of them all, and held by poor little Jetty Back! Jetty Back! Jetty Back, where did you light your lamp to-night?"

"I took the spark from a shingle roof, beneath which lay four little children asleep," she modestly answered. "It was a fierce, red spark, as you still may see, and it threatened to burn the dry roof and the old walls, and the children too. So I caught it up and bore it away, and the children sleep in safety while I shine gloriously here."

"And so," concluded Guy, "a good deed will shine, and glow, ages after evil and cruel ones are forgotten."

"That is a pretty story," said Aggie, contentedly, "and I am going to bed now to dream all night of the good fly, and her fadeless lamp. Good-night, dear Guy, don't forget that pretty story, for you must tell it again to-morrow."

CHAPTER IV.

But on the morrow neither the story of the fire-flies or any other was told, for late in the afternoon they arrived at Fort Leavenworth, which is situated on the western border of Missouri, and was then the last white settlement that travelers saw for many hundreds of miles.

All felt very sad the next morning when the train proceeded on its way. Many of them thought they were leaving civilization and its blessings forever behind, and as they looked toward the vast prairie of the West they remembered with a shudder how many had found a grave beneath its tall grass. But there was no delaying or turning back then, and so they slowly continued their way, pausing but once to give a farewell cheer for the flag that floated from the fort, and to look at their rifles and say, "We are ready for whatever may come!"

To Guy it seemed impossible that any one could long remain sad in the beautiful country they were entering upon. As far as the eye could reach lay a vast expanse of prairie, upon which the sunbeams lay like golden halo, making the long, rich grass of one uniform tint of pale green. Then a gentle breeze would come and ruffle the surface of this vast sea of vegetation, and immediately a hundred shades, varying from the deepest green to the lightest gold, would dance up and down each separate blade, producing the most wonderful chaos of colors. A great variety of the most lovely and delicate flowers, too, nestled beneath the grass, and sent forth sweet odors to refresh the traveler as he passed. Guy gathered them by handsful and gave them to Aggie, who wove them into long wreaths which she hung around the wagon, when she declared it looked like a fairy bower.

At midday they stopped to rest. The mules and oxen were turned out to graze on the luxuriant grass, and a small party of the men rode a short distance from camp in search of game. Guy would have greatly liked to accompany them, but as Mr. Harwood did not tell him to do so, he remained contentedly behind, assisting his mother to take care of the baby, and anxiously wondering when she would become strong and well, for she still looked as pale and weak as when they left W——.

He was speaking to his mother of this and hearing very thankfully her assurance that she felt better, if she did not look so, when Gus and George came up to him, and rapidly told him that their father had gone to the hunt and had left his powder flask behind and that their mother said he was to take it to them.

"But he is on horseback," said Guy, "and I should never be able to walk fast enough to overtake him. I'll go and speak to Mrs Harwood about it."

"Indeed you won't!" exclamed George, "she says you are not to bother her, but to go at once. You will be sure to meet papa, because he said they would not go farther than that little belt of cotton-wood trees which you see over there."

"Why, he did not go that way at all," cried Guy in astonishment. "He left the camp on the other side."

"Well, I know that," returned George, "but they were going toward that belt of trees, anyway. Didn't papa tell mamma so, Mrs. Loring?"

"Hallo! where has she gone to?"

"She went into the wagon before you began to speak to me," said Guy, not very well pleased with the cunning look in George's face.

"Oh, did she? All right! Here, take the flask and hurry along, or mamma will give it to you for lagging so. I wish I could go with you and see the hunt."

Guy was so fearful that he would do so whether he had permission or not, that he hurried away without farther thought, and was soon quite alone on the great prairie. I think he would not have gone so fast had he heard George's exultant laugh as he turned to Gus with the remark, "Isn't it jolly he's gone, but if you tell that I sent him away, I'll break your bones."

Gus had a very high regard for his

bones,—perhaps rather more than for the truth,—for he promised very readily to say nothing of what had passed, and indeed thought it an excellent joke, and laughed heartily.

Meanwhile Guy walked on in the direction George had pointed out to him, wondering as he forced his way through the tall grass, how Mr. Harwood could consider it enough of importance to send him with it. He walked a long distance without finding any traces of Mr. Harwood and his party, and looking back saw that the wagons appeared as mere specks above the grass. For a moment he felt inclined to turn back, but he remembered that his mother had told him always to finish anything he undertook to accomplish, and so stepped briskly forward quite determined to find Mr. Harwood if it was at all possible to do so.

It was a long time before he looked back again for he did not like to be tempted to return, and when he did so he was startled to find that the wagons had entirely disappeared. In great affright he looked north, east, west and south, but all in vain.

At first he ran wildly about, uttering broken ejaculations of alarm, then he sat down and burst into tears, it was so dreadful to be on that vast prairie alone. He soon grew calm for his tears relieved his overcharged heart. He arose and looked carefully around, and for the first time noticed that the trees which had seemed but a short distance from the camp, looked as far off as ever.

"It is plain," said he to himself, "that those trees are at a great distance. Of course, Mr. Harwood could calculate their distance though I could not, and would certainly never have ventured so far to hunt. George must have been mistaken."

Then he wondered that the flask he had so long carried in his hand had not oppressed him by its weight. With many misgivings he opened it, and found that he had been most basely, cruelly deceived. The flask was empty.

I think it is not surprising that Guy was very angry, and made some very foolish vows as to how he would "serve George out" if he ever gained the camp again. Ah! yes, if he ever gained it! But the question was how he was to do so, for the long prairie grass quite covered the tracks he had made and he was uncertain from what point he had come, and there was nothing in that great solitude to indicate it.

Oh, how Guy wished that the tall grass,

which he had thought so beautiful, was level with the earth, "Then I should be able to see the wagons," he thought, " but they have now moved on into some slight hollow, and I may never see them more."

Oh! how bitterly he reproached himself for his foolish trustfulness in George Harwood, and again for ever having persuaded his mother to undertake such a perilous journey. For even then he thought more of his mother's sorrow than his own danger, saying again and again: "I shall be lost, and my mother's heart will break. Oh, my dear, dear mother?"

"Well, well!" he exclaimed aloud, after spending a few moments in such sad reflections, "it is no use for me to stand here. There is one thing certain, I can meet nothing worse than death on this prairie if I go back, and if I stay here it will certainly come to me, so I will try to make for the wagons, and if I fail I shall know it is not for the want of energy."

So he forced his way again through the rank grass, this time with his back to the belt of trees, though he knew that they were growing by the side of water, for which he was eagerly wishing, for the sun was very hot, and as he had taken nothing since morning he was fast becoming faint with hunger and thirst.

At last the air grew cooler and a slight breeze sprang up, but although it refreshed Guy's weary body, it brought nothing but anguish to his mind, for he knew that the sun was setting.

In despair he lifted his voice and halloed wildly, crying for help from God and man, but no answer came, while still the sky grew a deeper blue, the sun a more glorious scarlet, till at last when it had gained its utmost magnificence, it suddenly dropped beneath the prairie, the green grass grew darker and darker, and at last lay like a black pall around poor Guy, as he stood alone in the awful solitude.

CHAPTER V.

For a time poor Guy sat upon the ground helpless, and hopeless, listening intently to the rustling movements of the numerous small animals, that wandered about seeking food; fearing to move, lest he should encounter a prairie wolf, or some other ferocious beast, and equally afraid to remain still, lest they should scent him there.

There was but one thing he could do, he felt then, and that was to put his trust in God, and entreat His guidance and protection. So, in the agony of his terror, he prostrated himself upon the ground, and offered up his petitions. The very act of praying comforted him, and when he lifted up his eyes, he was rejoiced to see a few bright stars shining in the sky.

"I think the moon will rise in about an hour," thought Guy, looking eagerly around, with a faint hope that she might even then be peering above the horizon; and truly, like a far off flame of fire, she seemed to hang above the prairie grass.

With great joy Guy waited for her to rise higher, and throw her glorious light across the wild, but she appeared almost motionless; and in much amazement at the singular phenomenon, he involuntarily walked rapidly toward the cause of his surprise, looking intently at it still. Suddenly he paused, and burst into a fit of laughter, exclaiming rapturously; "It is no moon; it is a camp fire! There! I can count one, two, three, of them, They are the fires of our own camp. Hurrah!"

In his excitement, he ran eagerly forward, shouting and laughing, but was suddenly tripped by the thick grass and thrown headlong. As he was quite severely hurt, he walked on much more soberly, but still at a brisk pace, towards the steadily brightening fires.

The moon he had so anxiously looked for, gave no indication of her presence in the heavens, and so Guy's progress was much retarded for the want of light, for the stars were often overwhelmed by great banks of clouds, and gave but a feeble ray at best.

"It is becoming very cold," thought Guy as he shivered in the rising wind, "I fear there is going to be a storm; Oh, what will become of me if it finds me here!"

Suddenly he paused, thinking for a moment that he heard shouting at a distance, but he listened for a long time, and heard no more, and continued his walk slowly and wearily, quite unable to repress his fast falling tears. He was so very tired, so hungry, and so cold, it was with the utmost difficulty he could force his way through the coarse grass. Very often too he was startled by some prowling animal, and thought with horror of all the tales he had read of boys being torn to pieces by wild beasts. He especially remembered one he had read in an old primer, of little Harry who was eaten by lions for saying "I won't" to his mother. He was thankful to know, that there were no lions on the prairies, and that he had never said "I won't," to his mother, but he very much feared he had said things just as bad, and that prairie wolves, or even a stray bear, might be lying in wait to devour him for it.

Just as he had reached this stage of his reflections, he fancied he heard some animal in pursuit of him. Without pausing even for an instant to listen, he set off at full speed toward the still glowing fires, till his precipitate flight was arrested by some obstacle, over which he fell, reaching the ground with a shock that almost stunned him.

As soon as he recovered his senses, he attemped to rise, but to his dismay, found that he could not stand. A sudden twinge of pain in his right ankle prostrated him, as quickly as if he had been shot.

He thought at first that his leg was broken, but after a careful examination, came to the conclusion that his ankle was sprained, but even a broken leg would not have been a greater misfortune then, for he was unable to walk, and was suffering the most excrutiating pain.

I think no one can imagine what poor Guy suffered, for the rest of that long night. There he lay helpless, in sight of the camp fires, but quite unable to reach them or to give any indications of his whereabouts to his friends. There he lay dying with pain, and hunger, and cold, yet suffering more in mind, than from all of these bodily evils, because he knew that his mother must know of his absence from the camp, and was wildly bemoaning the loss of her only child.

The long wished-for moon at length arose, hours after Guy had expected her, but too soon he thought when she made her appearance, for the camp fires grew dim beneath her rays, and he had to strain his aching eyes to see them at all. But he had not long to bemoan her presence, and to say, that she hid the light of home from him, for she soon plunged into a great bank of clouds; a fearful blast of wind swept by, and Guy was drenched with rain.

Oh, it was terrible, that passing storm! Short as it was, it appeared to Guy to last for hours, long after it had passed over him, he heard it wildly sweeping on, but as it grew fainter, and fainter, the calmness that came upon the night overpowered him, and he fell into a troubled sleep. It seemed but a short time before he again awoke, yet the grey dawn was struggling in the east, and the little birds were hopping from blade to blade of the wet grass twittering cheerily as if to thank God for the refreshing rain.

Poor Guy saw all this as if in a dream. He fancied he had been transformed into an icicle, and that some one had built a fire at his head, and was slowly melting him. He had no idea where he was, and talked constantly to his mother, whom he fancied was beside him, entreating her to put out the fire that was consuming him.

Suddenly he heard his name called, and realizing his position, and springing to his feet, in spite of his wounded limb, halloed loudly, waving his white handkerchief and signaling frantically to a horseman that appeared in the distance. For a few dreadful moments he was unheard, and unseen, then a shout of joy, answered his screams, and the horseman galloped rapidly toward him, and in a few minutes the poor boy lay fainting, but saved, in the arms of James Graham!

CHAPTER VI.

Guy knew no more for many hours. When he regained his senses, he found himself in Mrs. Harwood's wagon lying upon one of the divans. His mother was bending anxiously over him, and burst into a flood of joyful tears when she saw that he recognized her. Nothing could exceed Guy's joy at seeing her again though with traces of deep anxiety upon her face. Indeed, so delighted was he at his escape from death, that he was inclined to regard every one with favor! Even George Harwood, who a few days after his return to the camp, came to him, according to his father's instructions, to confess his unkindness and to ask pardon for the pain he had caused him.

"I just thought I would send you off on a fool's errand," said he, "but I never thought you would go so far, and frighten us nearly to death, and most kill yourself. I was so scared when you didn't come back I didn't know what to do. Father missed you, but thought you were somewhere about the wagons, and I dared not tell him you were not; but Gus turned coward during the afternoon, and told that I had sent you away—and *then* didn't I catch it?" and George grimaced most dolefully, pointing to poor Guy's sprained ankle, and declaring that the pain of that was nothing to what he had had in his back for days past.

Mrs. Loring came in then, and sent him away, as Guy had been ill with fever ever since his night's exposure, and could bear but little excitement. It was nearly two weeks before he could rise, and they had even then to carry him from place to place, because he could not bear his weight upon his wounded limb. It fretted him sorely when they camped at night, to see how hard she must have worked while he lay ill; yet he could but perceive that she looked better and stronger than she had done since his father's death, and joyfully felt that the excitement and toil of a journey across the plains would restore his mother to health, whatever might be the effect upon him.

How kind they all were to him during the time he was slowly regaining his health and strength. Aggie sat by him constantly, in her childish way telling him of the wonders she daily saw, or coaxing him to tell her some pretty tale. Mrs. Harwood always smiled upon him when she passed, and Amie and Carrie Graham often asked him to their wagon, and lent him books, or talked to him of the home they had left, and that which they hoped to find.

All the men missed Guy so much, he had always been so useful and good natured. Mr. Harwood daily said, that there should be a jubilee in camp when Guy got well again. But he recovered so gradually that he took his old place in the train by almost imperceptible degrees, and was at the end of a month as active as ever.

They were then on the borders of the Rio Platte, or Nebraska River, in the country of the Pawnee Indians. They were about to leave behind them the vast, luxuriant prairie, and enter upon what may more properly be called the plains. Guy was not sorry to see the thick grass become thinner and thinner, for he remembered that amid its clustering blades he had nearly lost his life, and therefore looked with much complacency upon the broad, shallow river, along which their course lay; the sandy loam beneath their feet, and the sand hills that arose like great billows of earth, rolling in regular succession over the level surface. George and Gus thought the country most dreary and wretched, and would scarcely believe Guy, when he told them of a desert called Sahara, that had not even a blade of grass upon it, save an occasional oasis, many miles apart, and which were often sought for, by the weary traveler, as he had himself sought the camp, during his terrible night on the prairie.

"It can't be worse than this," they eagerly contended, "I don't believe even Indians live here."

But they were soon convinced to the contrary, for a few days afterwards Guy started them by the exclamation " see the Indians! There are the Indians coming!"

George very boldly told them to "come on," but Gus went close to Guy, and declared that such mere specks as they saw in the distance couldn't be Indians; yet was suddenly most anxious to know whether they were cannibals, and if so, whether he looked a tempting morsel or not.

Guy could not help laughing at his questions, although he himself felt quite uneasy at the approach of the wild hunters of the prairies, which were seen rapidly drawing near to them. The men in the train formed a closer circle about the wagons, and hastily inspected their rifles, while Mr. Harwood gave them instructions how to proceed in case of an attack.

"That, however, he did not greatly apprehend, as they soon perceived the Indians were but a small party of middle-aged, or old men, and squaws, and it is seldom such a party attempts to molest any number of travelers.

However, Mr. Harwood thought it best to keep them at a safe distance, and when they approached within a hundred yards of the train, suddenly commanded them to halt by raising his right hand with the palm in front, and waving it backward and forward several times. They, upon this, stopped their horses, and consulted together a few moments, then fell into a posture indicative of rest. Then, Mr. Harwood raised his hand again and moved it slowly from right to left. This they understood to mean "who are you?" One of the oldest of them immediately replied by placing a hand on each side of the forehead, with two fingers pointing to the front, to represent the narrow, sharp ears of a wolf."

They are Pawnees, said Mr. Harwood. Ah! there is the chief making signs that they wish to talk with us."

A long conversation by means of signs, in the use of which the prairie Indians are very expert, was then carried on between Mr. Harwood and the old chief. Remembering his promise to Aggie, to protect her from the Indians, Guy went to Mrs. Harwood's wagon to assure her there was no danger, and that he would remain near, and then took a stand behind the wagon where he could see and hear all that passed.

He was soon joined by George and Gus, for Guy was always so calm and collected that they felt quite safe near him, though he was no stronger or older than themselves.

They all watched the Indians with much interest, and were surprised to see that instead of being giants, as accounts of their cruel and wonderful deeds had led them to expect, they were of medium height. In place of the horrible face, and the flaming eyes they had pictured, they saw the countenances of these Indians were intelligent, and although of course of a bright copper hue, were in some instances quite handsome. The hair of the men was very long, and streamed like black pennants, upon the wind. Their arms, shoulders, and breasts were quite naked, and their dress consisted only of deer skin, with a cloth wound around the lower part of the body. One or two were covered with buffalo robes, of which every warrior carries one, in which he wraps himself when cold.

Guy thought that the men as they sat proudly upon their beautiful horses, holding in their hands long bows made of the tough wood of the osage orange, which is as supple as elastic, looked very noble and fine. Their bows were about eight feet long and were wound around with the sinews of deer, and strung with a cord of the same. The arrows were about twenty inches long, of flexible wood, with a triangular point of iron at one end, and two feathers intersecting each other at right angles, at the opposite extremity."

This description Guy quoted to his companions, from a book he had once read, and they saw at once how perfectly true it was. While they were astonished at the appearance of the men, they were much diverted at that of the women. They were very short and ugly; each had her hair cut short, and they were dressed the same as the men with the addition of a skirt of dressed deer skin. Their faces were tattooed in the most uncouth devices, and altogether they appeared quite hideous, as they sat upon their horses, in the same position as the men, regarding with much interest the movements of their chief who had been made to understand that he might come alone to the train.

At first, he seemed doubtful about the propriety of such an act, but his wish for gain soon overcame his caution, and he rode up to Mr. Harwood, making many signs and protestations of friendship, which were returned most graciously. After a long series of compliments had passed between them, the old chief gave Mr. Harwood to understand that his people were hungry and needed sugar, corn, and many other things. Mr. Harwood replied by saying there were many deer upon the prairie, which they could kill, that they themselves had but little provision but would give them some beads, and bright paints, in token of the good feeling of the whites toward them.

At that the old man was delighted, for the Indians are very fond of beads and all kinds of ornaments, and of paints, with which they daub their faces and arms in the most grotesque manner, upon any grand occasion. But the old chief disdained to exhibit any satisfaction, and smoked the pipe, that had been offered him, in the most indifferent manner while the presents were being procured from the wagons.

When the old man had entered the camp, George and Gus thought it prudent to retreat to their mother's wagon, from whence, they could look out and see all that was going on. Aggie, on the contrary was so anxious to have a nearer view of the Indians, when she found them so much less terrible than she had imagined, that she begged her mother to allow her to stand with Guy outside the wagon, and after some little hesitation, Mrs. Harwood permitted her to do so.

When Guy lifted the little girl from the wagon, the savage gave a grunt of surprise, and gazed for a long time upon her with such evident admiration that Guy was greatly afraid he would take a fancy to carry her off. But Aggie, herself entertained no such fears, and after looking at the old man curiously for some little time, approached him slowly and examined his strange dress, the circular shield covered with buffalo hide that was strapped on his left arm, and the formidable war-club that lay at his side. It was made of a stone, about two pounds in weight, round which a withe of elastic wood was bound, being held in its place by a groove which had been formerly cut in the stone. The two ends of the withe formed a handle about fourteen inches long, and were bound together with strips of buffalo hide, which rendered it strong and firm, totally preventing it from either splitting down, or breaking when used, as no doubt it often was, with great force, upon the heads of unfortunate enemies.

The old chief allowed Aggie to examine all those things with the greatest good nature, and when she touched his quiver of arrows, and asked him to give her one, he grunted assent; so she took the prettiest one, and after admiring it for some time, nodded and smiled, and walked toward Guy with the prize in her hand. But immediately the Indian darted to his feet, frowning with anger, and sprang toward the frightened child. Mr. Harwood and most of the men believed for the moment that he was indeed about to attempt to carry her off, and with loud voices bade him stand back, and levelled their rifles upon him, to enforce obedience. The old man raised his hand, and immediately the whole force on the prairie commenced galloping toward them.

"Aggie give him his arrow!" cried Guy at this juncture, "he misunderstood you; he thinks you have stolen his arrows! Give it to him."

She did so, the old man released her, and she fled to the wagon like a frightened deer. With a few expressive gestures Guy explained to the Indian the mistake that had been made, and at the same time it became evident to Mr. Harwood and his party. The chief signaled to his party to retire, and in less time than it has taken to describe it, peace was restored; whereas but for Guy's presence of mind a terrible battle might have followed Aggie's innocent freak.

But, notwithstanding that peace had been restored, they were all glad when the chief took up his presents and went back to his motley followers, and even more so, when they put their horses to their utmost speed, and returned to their lodges; where no doubt they gave to their tribe an astounding account of the adventure of their chief in the camp of the white man.

CHAPTER VII.

For some time after the encounter with the Indians, which happily ended so peacefully, the train moved on without meeting with any adventures. George and Gus thought the days passed very drearily, and longed for some excitement, but Guy was altogether too busy to feel dull. Mrs. Harwood's baby was quite sick, and as Mrs. Loring's time was fully taken up in attending to him, Guy had double work to do.

You would be surprised if I should tell you half that he did. Of all the fires he built; the oxen he fed; the water he carried, and even the breakfasts and suppers he helped to cook. And he did it all in the best manner of which he was capable too. Although the first biscuits he made were heavy, the next were light as down, for he inquired into the cause of his failure and rectified it, and by doing that in every case he soon learned to do perfectly all that he undertook.

Most children would have thought the life of constant toil which Guy led very wretched indeed; but he did not, for he had daily the gratification of perceiving that the great object of their journey across the plains was being gradually accomplished; his mother's health was slowly becoming strengthened, by every step they took toward the snowy mountains, beyond which lay the fruitful valleys in which they hoped to find a home.

But, as the days passed by, they greatly feared that one of their number would never reach there; the baby boy grew worse. The cooling breezes that brought health to his weakly sister, seemed fraught with death for the lately blooming boy. Guy was greatly saddened by the sufferings of the child, and by the grief of its parents, and shuddered when he saw the bones of animals which lay by thousands bleaching upon the desert, and once was filled with horror on coming across a human skull, which the prairie wolves had dragged from some shallow grave, and separated far from its kindred bones. The idea that the body of the poor little baby should meet such a fate, filled him with sorrow, and although it had always seemed to him a natural and peaceful thing that the temple of clay should rest under its native dust, after the flight of the soul, he thought that the Indian mode of sepulture, of which they saw examples every day, by far the best.

Very often they saw a curious object in

the distance, and two of the party, riding forward to examine it, would report an Indian place of burial. Guy had himself gone forward once and found, to his surprise, two forked poles, some six or eight feet high, supporting something wrapped in a blanket. This something was a dead Indian, who in this strange position, with his weapons in his hands, was waiting his summons to the "happy hunting grounds."

On his return to the train, Guy hastened to find Aggie, to tell her of what he had seen. She was listening very attentively, when George ran up, exclaiming: "Look at the rats! there are thousands of rats on the plains!"

Aggie looked in the direction indicated by her brother, and crying: "Oh, the dreadful rats," was about to run away, when Guy stopped her, telling her, laughingly, that they were the wonderful little prairie dogs, of which they had heard so much.

Truly enough when she gained courage to look at the little animals, she saw that although they at first sight resembled rats, on closer inspection they appeared even more like squirrels. The children were greatly entertained by watching their quick, active movements, as they darted about through the low grass. A very busy community they appeared to be, and with plenty to gossip about. To Aggie's delight Guy pretended to translate their quick, chirruping barks into our own language. Some he said were telling how a monster rattlesnake had come to visit them without any invitation, and that the only food he would eat, was the youngest and fattest of their families; and that their constant intruders, the owls, had the same carnivorous tastes, besides which they rendered themselves particularly disagreeable, by standing in the doors and staring at every dog that went by, and even preventing the entrance of visitors, to the great distress of all the belles and beaux in town.

All this may have been very true, for the excited little creatures talked so continuously that I am sure they must have had some grievance, and the children thought it must be the owls that stood solemnly at the entrance of many of the burrows. They did not see the rattlesnakes, so even Aggie somewhat doubted the tales of their ferocity, which Guy said the little prairie dogs related.

But although these little creatures were such chatterers, they appeared very industrious, for many hillocks of sand indicated where their homes were burrowed. Each little hole was occupied by a pair of dogs, one of which was often seen perched on the apex like a sentinel. But like many other sentinels, they appeared on the watch for danger, not to combat, but to avoid it, for they darted like a flash into their holes whenever a lean, prowling wolf stalked near them, or even a prairie hen flew by.

"I wish you would tell us a story about prairie dogs," said Aggie to Guy, that evening when they were gathered around the camp-fire.

"I am afraid it is impossible for me to do that," he replied, "for very little seems to be known about them. Naturalists have never paid much attention to them, curious as they are."

"But the Indians must know something about them," said Gus.

"Yes, I suppose so," returned Guy, for before the white man came to annoy them, they had nothing to do but to watch animals and learn their habits, that they might know which were fit for food, and which was the easiest way of killing them. Ah, yes, now that I have been thinking about it, I do remember a story that the Indians tell about the prairie dogs!"

"Oh tell it!" cried Aggie, eagerly; Gus seconded the request, and even George drew nearer, for Guy had a great reputation as story teller in the camp.

"It is rather a long tale," said he, "but the Indians say, a true one. It happened years and years ago when each animal understood the language of all others, and men conversed with them as readily as with themselves.

"In those days each tribe had its sorcerers, or wise men, who pretended to cure not only all diseases but to control the destinies of men. They were accordingly held in great veneration by their simple-minded dupes, as are their few descendants, which even at this day practice in a lesser degree the arts of their forefathers.

" Well, it happened that when these men were more powerful among the tribes than the chiefs themselves, that they combined together to wrest from the hands of these the commands that they held, in order that they might hold the people both in bodily and mental subjection. There had for a long time existed a tradition among them, that when a daughter of a chief—an only child,—should love a brave of an unfriendly tribe, they would have power to change her into a flower or animal, and unless the brave should find the means within ten moons, or months, to brake the enchantment, she would die, and with her every chieftain and his family. Accordingly these wicked sorcerers found constant pretexts for involving the tribes in war, especially if they supposed that the only daughter of a chieftain loved a brave of another tribe; but for many years all their arts were in vain, for the Indians were so passionate and revengeful that immediately an affront was given or received, violent hatred vanquished love, and the chiefs and their families were saved.

"The sorcerers were almost in despair of ever obtaining the entire authority they craved, when it came to pass that two rival tribes met upon the plains, and as was usual in such cases, a battle was fought. The Ohoolee tribe were victorious, and killed many of the Gheelees and also took many of them prisoners. Among the latter, was the only daughter of the chief Sartahnah, the beautiful Mahdrusa.

"Great was the consternation of her tribe, for this maiden was held more precious by them, than a hundred braves. She was more graceful than the fairest flower that grew upon the prairie; her hair was longer than the grass by the riverside and blacker than the night; her eyes were like those of the young fawn, and her voice was sweeter than a breeze laden with the song of birds. There was not a chieftain or brave of the Gheelee's but would have laid down his life for her, and great was the grief and shame that befell them when she was taken captive by the Ohoolees.

"From that day there was continual war waged between the two tribes. The Ohoolees acted on the defensive, the Gheelees on the offensive. Never a week passed but that a party of braves went forth to attempt the rescue of the beautiful Mahdrusa from the lodges of the enemy. The chief, her father, to increase if possible the zeal of the braves promised her hand to him who should deliver her. There was great rejoicing when this was made known, for all loved Mahdrusa, though she cared for none. Her rescue was attempted with a thousand times more eagerness than before, and one day Anoctah, the bravest of all the Gheelees, led her in triumph to her father's wigwam and demanded his reward.

"Mahdrusa heard him with dismay, and clasping her father's knees, sank down before him, and entreated him to give Anoctah some other treasure.

"The old chief told her that was impossible, and Mahdrusa wept so loudly that the whole tribe gathered about the lodge and asked what had befallen the beautiful daughter of Sartahnah. But she would say nothing, yet wept continually, so that the sorcerers said the spirit of the rivers was within her, and that they alone could deliver her from it.

"Now these men had reasoned together

over her strange malady, and said, 'She mourns so much over her betrothal to Anoctah because she loves a brave of an unfriendly tribe. Let us then take her from her father, and place her in the great medicine lodge where we can work our enchantments upon her, and make ourselves rulers of all the tribes.'

"So in the night they took her from her father's wigwam into the great medicine lodge, which was hung about with the herbs they used in their incantations, and had in the centre a great heap of stones, within which was a fire burning.

"Beside these stones, which were kept constantly hot, they made Mahdrusa sit down, and while she still wept, her tears fell upon the stones, and a great vapor arose, which the sorcerers condensed upon clay vessels into drops of water as pure as crystal, and with them and the herbs that hung around, made a decoction so powerful that when they had forced Mahdrusa to drink it, she lost all power and reason, and her spirit lay passive in the hands of her tormentors.

"'We will take it from her body,' said they, 'and place it where no brave will ever discover it.

"'Let it fly to the centre of the wild rose,' said one. But the others demurred, saying her lover would certainly seek it there.

"'Better hide it under the thick skin of the buffalo,' said another.

"'No!' they answered, 'the brave that Mahdrusa loves must be a fearless hunter, therefore his arrow would bring her forth.'

"In short, they talked of every flower and beast on the prairie, but found in all some fault, until the most cunning of all mentioned the prairie dogs. 'No one would look for her in their miserable holes,' said he, 'and they are such chatterers that the magpies, themselves, would not have patience to listen to them.'

"So it was agreed that her spirit should dwell as a prairie dog, and before long out sprang one from a reeking cauldron of herbs, and they took it to the holes of the prairie dogs and left it there, placing beside it a terrible serpent, that all others might be afraid to approach it, and an owl at the door, as a sentinel that would stand looking patiently for an enemy both night and day, and never breathe to the gossips around her the tale of the princess that was prisoned within.

"And that was how the rattlesnake and owl became sharers in the homes of the prairie dogs, and it was with these awful companions that the spirit of Mahdrusa spent many weary days. Meanwhile her body lay in the medicine lodge of her people, and the sorcerers said that her soul had ascended to the stars, where, in ten moons, she would be purified from her sin and return to her body, or that it would die, and moulder away.

"This news soon spread over the prairies, but the brave that Mahdrusa loved would not believe it. He knew the wicked desires of the sorcerers, and believed that she was a flower on the prairie, and that he was appointed to rescue her.

"So he went forth and cut down every flower that he found, and he toiled so ceaselessly that before two moons had passed not a blossom remained, and still he found not his beautiful Mahdrusa. Then he made a strong bow, and arrows that could not miss the mark, and he slew the beasts of the prairie by hundreds, yet he could not find his love. And so nine moons passed by, and Mahdrusa was still in her horrible captivity, and the brave that sought her was bowed down as if by years, with the weight of his sorrow, and his body was so steeped in the blood of the animals he had slain that he was redder than clay, and his descendants continue so to this very time. All the beasts of the prairie had he slain in his terrible anger, and all the people had fled to the mountains for food, thither he thought he would follow them, and he sat down upon a ridge of sand, to strengthen his bow, and sharpen his arrows, when, lo! quite unmindful of him, a thousand little creatures he had fancied too insignificant to notice, sprang forth from their holes, and gathered in groups for their daily gossip.

"They angered him so greatly by their chatter that he placed an arrow on his bow to fire amongst them, when his hand was stayed by hearing a curious tale that a gay young dog was telling.

"'She lives next to my mother's lodge,' said he, 'and the poor thing never appears either to eat or drink. I took her a delicate slice of cactus myself, but I dropped it in a terrible fright, for a great serpent darted towards me, and an owl sprang forward and devoured my youngest brother before he had time to utter a squeak.'

"The brave rejoiced when he heard these words, and springing up, went in search of the captive prairie dog. Many weary days he sought in vain. He asked of her whereabouts from every insect he met, but none could give him any information, and the prairie dogs, under the spell of the sorcerers, were silent—on that topic, at least.

"There was but a day left in which he could act. Almost in despair, he wandered about the prairie dog town, vainly looking for his love.

"At last he remembered that a queer old woman whom he had met, while hunting one day, had told him that she was his guardian fairy, and had given him two little pieces of stone which he was to strike together if ever he was in great trouble, and she would appear and help him.

"He had taken but little notice of the old woman at the time, supposing her to be a conjurer or evil worker, and he had dropped the little stones into his pouch, where they had long lain forgotten. Without daring to hope that they would be of any use, he took them out, and struck them together. A tiny spark of fire fell from them upon some dry grass at his feet, a flame sprang up, and lo! out of it stepped the old woman he sought.

"'So you have called me at last!' said she, 'what is it that I shall do?'

"'Lead me, kind fairy, to the hiding place of the beautiful Mahdrusa,' he replied.

"So she went before him to a part of the prairie that, in all his wanderings, he had not visited. But, strangely enough, before his feet the grass turned into briars, through which he only with the greatest difficulty could force his way. Every timid hare became a wolf, each gentle fawn a raging buffalo, but the brave went on undaunted, brandishing his war-club, and keeping his formidable foes at bay. Never for a moment did he allow fear to gain possession of him for he knew if he did he should be lost. It was only faith and courage that could carry him safely through that enchanted ground.

"'Stop!' cried the fairy, when he had

passed unscathed through a thousand dangers. 'Mahdrusa is before you!'

"But before he could look for her, the owl flew like a fierce hawk in his face, and pecked at his eyes, and the rattlesnake sprang upon him burying its deadly fangs into his arm. The brave almost lost his courage then, but he heard Mahdrusa, though in the voice of a prairie dog, entreating him to save her. He caught the serpent in his hands, and seizing its jaws, tore it asunder, and wrapped its writhing body around his wound, while at the same moment the fairy called up a terrible wind that blew the owl far away, and to the arms of the young warrior, the little prairie dog that held the soul of Mahdrusa.

"So was half the task of the lover accomplished; yet all his toil would be in vain if he could not before the moon set that night place her soul in the body it had before tenanted. But he was many leagues from the lodge in which it lay, and he knew that by his own power he could not hope to reach it in time, so he called upon the good fairy again, and she turned a rabbit into a fleet courser that bore the lover and the enchanted maiden, over the prairie with the swiftness of wind.

"The moon was but a few inches, it appeared, above the horizon, when they reached the lodge. By command of the sorcerers all the people had returned from the mountains to see whether the spirit of Mahdrusa would come from the stars, or her body, which all this time had lain as if in a deep sleep, take upon itself the signs of death. All were gathered in the great lodge. The cauldron of herbs from which the enchanted prairie dog had emerged was boiling over the fire, and around it the sorcerers were standing. Before them lay the body of the beautiful Mahdrusa, and beside it stood her father and Anoctah.

"Into the lodge, into the midst of all the people, the young brave sprang! The warriors of the Gheclees raised their war clubs when they saw one of the hated Ohoolees, but the young brave cried, 'strike me not, for I bear the soul of Mahdrusa!'

"Then they all fell back and Anoctah said, 'Restore it to her body, and she shall be thine, if she loves thee better than me.'

"But the sorcerers sprang upon him, and tried to tear the little prairie dog from his bosom, but the fairy cried:—

"'Hold her with thy right hand into the cauldron and she shall be saved!'

"So he broke away from the sorcerers and plunged the enchanted one into the boiling cauldron, unheading the agony he suffered or the cries of the little animal he held, and in a moment the moon plunged beneath the horizon; Mahdrusa arose from her long sleep; the sorcerers fell into the boiling cauldron and were consumed; and all the people shouted for joy, and with one accord cried that the Ohoolees should from henceforth be their brothers, and the young brave who had rescued Mahdrusa, their chieftain, when her father was called to the happy hunting grounds.

"The next day the marriage of the young brave and Mahdrusa was celebrated with great splendor. And, behold, after the ceremony was over, a beautiful young maiden stood in the place where the old woman had been.

"'I too was enchanted by those wicked sorcerers, and condemned to wear the form of an old woman until I should make two young hearts perfectly happy. I have completed my task to-day.'

"Then Anoctah who had been very sorrowful, looked up, and seeing the beautiful maiden, forgot his love for Mahdrusa, and entreated the stranger to be his wife.

"She loved him well and consented, and thus made a third heart joyful as those of the young Ohoolee brave and his beautiful Mahdrusa.

"And they lived happily together all their lives," quoted Aggie, from the fairy tales she had heard. "Why, Guy, that *was* a long story," she added yawning, "and it has made me so sleepy I shall go to bed. Good-night!"

"Good-night," returned Guy, not very well pleased that she should be so sleepy, and fearing that his story must have been very stupid as well as long. Perhaps it was because of this, that he sat down by the fire again when she was gone instead of going to bed as he usually did, and it was from sitting there that he got into trouble on the following day, and to tell you what his ·trouble was shall be the duty of the next chapter.

CHAPTER VIII.

"I say," said George, slapping Guy on the shoulder, the moment after his father bade them "good-night" and went to his wagon, telling them to go to theirs, "I say, I have got the best thing to tell you, and we'll have the greatest fun, if you don't turn sneak and try to get out of it."

"I'm not likely to turn sneak!" retorted Guy very indignant that he should be thought capable of such a thing. "What are we to have such fun at? I don't think you will find that I shall shirk it."

Now, Guy never would have said that without knowing what George's fun was to be, had he not been vexed at Aggie's cool reception of his story, and at some other things that had happened through the day. He was in a very restless, dissatisfied temper, and, as many other boys do under those circumstances, he felt like doing any wild thing that was suggested to him, without inquiring whether it was right or wrong.

George saw that, and, greatly delighted, said: "I told Gus I didn't believe you would back out, and we will have such a jolly time! You know there are numbers of antelopes on the plains here, and I heard James Graham say this morning, that there would be sure to be a great many of them go down to that little creek to drink just as soon as the moon rose."

"Well," said Guy, wondering greatly what the herd of antelopes had to do with their fun.

"Well," returned George, "I have been reading a book that tells all about hunting them. That was what I was doing when pa thought me so studious to-day, and I found out how to hunt them at night, and it's just as easy as can be. You have only to creep up to them silently, and you can shoot them down by dozens."

"Like partridges?" commented Guy, in a tone of doubt.

"You needn't laugh at what I say," returned George. "You can ask Gus if it isn't so, and if you don't believe him, I'll show you the book."

"Oh! I believe it all, of course!" said Guy, hastily; "but I don't see what difference it makes to us, for we have nothing to hunt antelopes with."

"There are plenty of guns in the wagon," said George, in a low voice, "and I don't see why we shouldn't use them."

Guy was greatly startled at this speech, for Mr. Harwood had told all the boys never to touch one of the guns. He reminded George of that, but he only laughed, and began a glowing account of the glorious time they would have in creeping toward the creek, in the moonlight, and shooting down the antelopes as they bent their heads to drink.

Guy's imagination was highly excited by George's words, and from being the most unwilling, he became the most anxious that the midnight hunt should be attempted, quite forgetting Mr. Harwood's commands in thinking of the triumph they might have in the morning, in exhibiting two or three dead antelopes.

He readily assented to George's proposition, that they should then proceed to the wagon, and choose their guns. No inducements or threats, even to the breaking of his bones, would induce Gus to touch one.

"Then," said George, "you shall carry this small hatchet, and a knife, so that we shall be able to cut the horns and tails off the antelopes that we can't bring home with us. I don't suppose we shall be able to carry more than one apiece."

After securing their guns, they left the camp very cautiously, each one going a different way, and all meeting at a point about a quarter of a mile from the camp, on the banks of the little stream, where they expected the antelopes would come to drink.

They stayed there in silence for some time, for Guy, remembering his former experience on the prairie, was afraid to venture for even a moment out of sight of the camp-fires. But at last they all became so impatient at remaining so still and seeing nothing, that they ventured, very cautiously, a little farther up the stream. Guy took the lead, and very often would stop, and motion to his companions to do likewise, whenever he fancied he heard any noise.

Thus two very tiresome hours passed away, and Gus was very crossly protesting against staying any longer, when Guy motioned him very eagerly to be still, and with great triumph pointed to a number of animals that, one by one, very slowly and cautiously, were going down to the water to drink.

They were very slender and graceful, about the size of a small deer, and covered with coarse, wiry hair, and bearing upon their small, well-formed heads a pair of branching horns.

They descended to the water, without exhibiting any signs of suspicion or fear, for the boys, quite by accident, had got to the leeward of them—that is, where the wind would not pass from them to the antelopes, and give to the keen animals notice of their presence.

"Now," whispered Guy, excitedly, "wait until you see them stoop their heads to drink, and then fire at them! Now—ready!"

Both boys raised their guns and fired. There was a terrible concussion. Both were thrown flat upon their backs, with the idea that their heads, or at least their noses, were shot off, and away stampeded the antelopes, as fast as their slender legs would carry them.

Gus began to howl and cry most wildly, believing that his brother and Guy were both killed. They, however, soon convinced him that they were both alive, by rising, each declaring his nose was broken, and pointing to the flowing blood as proof of it.

George was terribly enraged, chiefly at the gun, which he declared had "kicked" him. Guy, on his part, was very much vexed with George, for having brought him on such a profitless adventure; but though he was suffering very much from his rashness, the whole thing appeared to him so ridiculous, that he laughed long and heartily.

"I believe you would laugh if you were dying," grumbled George, as they stood together by the side of the creek, washing their face. "Pretty figures we shall make to-morrow, sha'n't we? And pa will give it to you to-morrow, too, for taking the guns."

"You told me to do it!" retorted Guy, sullenly, but quite alarmed at the thought of Mr. Harwood's impending wrath, as well as angry at himself for having done anything to incur it.

George answered him very rudely, and then followed a quarrel between the two, which was at last brought to an abrupt termination by a terrible scream from Gus. They looked toward him, and saw, with horror, an immense panther, but a short distance off, making ready for a spring.

The boys were transfixed with horror, as they saw his glaring eyes fixed upon them.

They saw him crouch like an immense cat, preparing to spring upon its prey. They saw a sudden flash of fire before their eyes, heard the report of a gun, and, with as much fear as joy, beheld the terrible monster spring high into the air, and fall to the ground, tearing up the ground with its claws, and foaming at the mouth, in agony. Another shot ended its struggles and its life together.

The boys uttered cries of joy for their delivery from the terrible death with which the panther had threatened one, or perhaps even all, of them; but they were very much frightened to see that their deliverer was Mr. Harwood.

He looked at them very sternly and said—

"You may be very thankful that I heard the reports of your guns and came in search of you, or your disobedience might have been punished most fearfully."

With great sorrow and shame they felt that his words were true, as they stood beside the dead panther, and looked at his long claws, and the firm white teeth in his large mouth.

Gus burst into tears, and said he knew the horrible creature was making straight for him, and eagerly assured his father that he would never disobey him again in his life.

George and Guy were quite ready to make the same promise, but Mr. Harwood looked so stern that they dared not speak to him, and Guy felt utterly wretched when, instead of scolding him, Mr. Harwood looked at him very sorrowfully, and said:

"I am disappointed in you, Guy! I thought I could trust you."

"The next thing, I heard the reports of the guns, and immediately surmised where you were. I was so anxious about you, that I would not call one of the others, but came immediately in pursuit of you, and it is well that I did."

"How was the baby, when you left?" asked the conscience-stricken Guy.

"Dying," returned Mr. Harwood, emphatically.

Guy waited to hear no more, but darted forward, reaching the camp some minutes before his companions. He saw that several in the train were up, and some called after him, asking where he had been. Without stopping to answer them, he ran on to Mrs. Harwood's wagon, and seeing it all alight within, sprang to the front, and hastily putting the canvas door aside, asked how the baby was.

His mother came over to him, crying and wringing her hands—

"Oh, Guy!" she cried, "where have you been? How wicked you were to leave us so, when the baby was dying!"

Guy knew not what to say—he had no excuse to offer, for he never thought of putting the blame on George. He, therefore, kept silent, and in a most miserable state of mind, followed Mr. Harwood and his sons to the camp.

Gus kept close to his father all the way, crying out every minute or two that he saw another panther, and at last asking how it was that their absence from camp was discovered.

"The baby was very ill," answered Mr. Harwood, gravely. "He was in convulsions, and your mother wanted to put him in a hot bath. I went to call Guy to help us, and then found you were gone."

"And what did you do then?" asked Gus.

"Oh, mother!" he cried, "is he dead!"

"Yes," she answered. "He died while you were laughing and sporting. I should think you would never enjoy yourself again, while you can remember that."

Guy looked at the little babe, lying dead on its mother's lap, and thought, indeed, that he never should be happy again. Aggie added to his distress by looking at him sternly, with her widely-opened eyes, and crying:

"Go away, you bad, bad boy! I will never love you again."

"And Mr. Harwood will never trust me," thought Guy, bitterly, as he left the wagon, and passed Mr. Harwood and his sons, who were about to enter it.

Guy slept but very little that night; in the first place, his bruised face was very painful, and he was, besides, haunted by the remembrance of Mr. Harwood's reproachful glance, when he had said he had been deceived in him; and he wondered if he would carry into execution the threat he had made before they left home, and greatly feared that he would, for he felt that he had been quite disobedient, and seemingly ungrateful enough, to be left alone on the prairie.

The train did not move on as early the next morning as usual, for the poor little baby was buried upon the banks of the little stream where the boys had so nearly lost their lives.

Guy thought he had never witnessed so sad a scene as when they laid the beautiful baby, that looked as pure and sweet as a white lily, in the rough coffin that some of the young men had hastily made, and carried him to a lonely spot, that perhaps no feet had ever trod before, and, breathing a prayer over him, left him to his long sleep, far from the place of his birth, or that for which his kindred were bound, and where never a tear would be dropped above him, or a sigh breathed.

Guy's only comfort was, and, perhaps, too, that of the poor baby's father and mother, that he could not be quite alone, even when they left him, for God would watch over him; and he could not but rejoice that they had not been forced to leave him in the shifting sands of the desert, but that a green tree bent over him, and grass would spring above the sod in which he lay.

Poor little Aggie was quite brokenhearted at the loss of her poor little playfellow, and, quite forgetting her anger went to Guy for comfort.

After he had said all he could to cheer her, he told her of his own troubles, and how sincerely sorry he was, for having disobeyed her father. Aggie listened very attentively, and at last said:

"Perhaps papa will forgive you. I know he will, if you go to him and tell him how sorry you are, and promise him you will never be so wild and disobedient again."

"That I will," said Guy readily. "I

would do anything to merit his kindness once more."

But it was several days before Guy could summon courage to speak to Mr. Harwood, who treated him very coldly, seldom asking him to do anything, and never intrusting the care of even the slightest article to him. Guy every day grew more and more miserable, while Gus and George congratulated themselves upon their father's silence, and almost forgot that they had ever incurred his displeasure.

"But, if the baby hadn't died, wouldn't he have 'whaled' us, though!" ejaculated George, one day.

Guy was shocked and surprised to hear him speak so lightly, and, without more ado, left him, and going to Mr. Harwood, told him how grieved he was for his disobedience, and begged him to forgive him, and restore him to his confidence again.

"I will forgive you, Guy," said Mr. Harwood, kindly; "but I cannot place any trust in you again, until you show yourself worthy of it.

"I will show myself worthy!" exclaimed Guy, firmly. "I will, indeed, Mr. Harwood, and at the same time show my gratitude for your kindness."

And scarcely a week passed before Guy fulfilled his promise.

CHAPTER IX.

"I believe it is snowing over yonder," cried Aggie to Guy one day, pointing to the west, where, truly enough, as far as the eye could reach, the earth appeared perfectly white.

"It does look like snow," returned Guy, looking intently in the direction she indicated, "but it is now June, and we certainly ought not to encounter such a fall as that appears to be, besides, there is a perfect glare of sunshine there! Ah, I have it! That is not snow, but alkali!"

"What is alkali?" asked Aggie. "Is it cold! Will it melt?"

"I don't know," answered Guy, "let us ask Mr. Graham, he will be able to tell us all about it."

So that very evening when the train stopped to encamp for the night, they waited until Mr. Graham had finished his work, and Guy had done all that was required of him, and then went to the campfire of the Grahams.

They were very warmly welcomed, for both Guy and Aggie were great favorites of them all, and after they were all quietly seated, Guy pointed to the desert of alkali that shone like crystal beneath the beams of the moon, and asked Mr. Graham if he could tell them of what it was composed, and how it came there.

"Of the last I can say nothing," returned Mr. Graham, "except that it was placed there by an all-wise Creator for some good purpose. The substance itself is a sulphate of soda, and is generally found near sulphur, and soda springs. A fall of rain usually brings it forth from the earth it impregnates in great quantities, and it looks very beautiful. The white particles often assume the most delicate shapes, like flakes of snow for instance, or most delicate leaves, and ferns."

"I shall be very glad when we get there," said Aggie, "I shall think we are passing a winter in fairy lands."

"Then I am afraid you will think it a very disagreeable winter," returned Mr. Graham, laughing.

"Why?" asked Aggie, opening wide her eyes in astonishment. "Is it cold there? I thought that the sun shone as warmly there as it does here."

"So it does," replied Mr. Graham. "It will not be of the weather that you will complain, but of what you call the beautiful snow."

"Ah! yes, perhaps the glare will hurt my eyes."

"I think it very likely, Aggie," said Amy Graham, "but my brother was not thinking of that, but of something much worse. These alkali salts are very poisonous, and often kill people if they are partaken of even slightly."

"Indeed!" ejaculated Aggie and Guy at once.

"I'll never touch them!" continued the latter, "and I am so sorry I can't, because I thought it would be so nice to eat some, as if it was snow."

"I should never think of eating it," said Guy. "And I think Aggie would not when she had once seen what kind of a substance it is," said Mr. Graham, "for it looks much more like powdered washing-soda than snow, and tastes more like it too."

"Then I am sure I wouldn't take enough even to make my mouth taste badly!" exclaimed Aggie, with a gesture of disgust.

"I thought the same at one time," said Mr. Graham, "yet it was only a very short time afterwards that I was nearly killed by partaking of it."

"How?" cried both the children, eagerly. "Do tell us about it, Mr. Graham."

"Certainly I will," he answered, kindly. "I believe I have told you before that this is not the first time I have been across the plains. I made my first trip before gold was discovered in California, and when few people thought of going there.

"There was then no well defined route such as we have been following, and when we reached the alkali desert we lost trace of any road, and had to depend entirely upon our reasoning powers for guidance."

"Hadn't you any compass?" asked Guy.

"Certainly," replied Mr. Graham, "but

as we were rather uncertain which direction we ought to take, it was not of much use to us. Before a week was over, both ourselves and the cattle were quite worn down with our tiresome march across the glaring, blinding desert. Our condition daily grew worse, for all sickened, and suffered dreadfully for want of water, for there was none to be found but that which was impregnated with soda. Many of the people drank it, and became very sick; the weary oxen quaffed it from the little pools, formed by the rain, by the wayside, and daily two or three died, and we were compelled to leave them to bleach as white as the alkali around them. For my part, I drank no water for days; enduring the agonies of thirst in silence, and praying that we might soon find relief. One day, one of my comrades died, he had borne the torture attending abstinence as long as possible, and then had drank to repletion, and been poisoned. There had been a heavy shower, and he had been quite unable to resist the temptation it offered. Two days after, it rained again, and I was almost as imprudent as my friend had been, and was immediately taken so ill that I feared I should share his resting-place. I never shall forget how rejoiced I was when we got into a pure atmosphere and healthy soil again, but it was weeks, yes, even months, before the effects of my poisoned draught passed entirely away."

"Dear me," cried Aggie, in dismay, "are there no June springs in the alkali desert! Oh, dear! dear! just think of having come so far just to be poisoned!"

"We will see that you do not drink after a shower," said Mr. Graham, laughing. "But even the little birds could do that here. And indeed there will be no necessity for you to do so, as several springs have been discovered since the time I spoke of."

"I wish you hadn't told me about it," said Aggie, sadly, "I shall think all the time of the poor creatures that have been poisoned. I don't like to hear of such dreadful things, even if they are true. I would a great deal rather hear a pretty story. Miss Carrie, won't you tell me one?"

"My brother has told you of something that once happened to him," she replied, readily, "and now, if you like, I will relate a little adventure that befel me when I was a little girl."

"Oh! that will be splendid, Miss Carrie. Do tell us all about it."

"I must tell you, in the first place," began Miss Graham, when she had drawn Aggie nearer to her side, so that she should not lose one word she was about to say, "that I was not at all a good little girl at the time the event I am going to tell you of, took place, and you must not, therefore, be surprised to hear of any naughty actions I used to do.

"My favorite ones were those by which I could frighten people. Nothing used to delight me so much as to tell ghost stories to my younger brothers and sisters and leave them without explaining them, when often the poor little creatures would become nearly convulsed with terror, and my mother would find great trouble in quieting them. I had often been scolded, and even whipped for my malicious mischief but all to no purpose, and at last no notice was taken of me, and I thought my father and mother had made up their mind to let me tell horrible stories until I was tired of them. My parents often went out in the evening to the theatre, or some party and on such occasions it was my usual practice to coax my brother Charlie, and sister Amy into the dining room with me, while the nurse put my youngest brother to bed. When I had, by dint of threats, and persuasions, got them into the room, I would make them sit by the fire suddenly put out the candles, and begin some dreadful story. Generally the nurse came in the middle of it and carried them away to bed, where they would cower under the blankets and tremble at every sound."

"I know," interrupted Aggie, "I used to do that after George had told me stories. But did you believe what you used to tell them?"

"'No, my love,' 'although I have indeed told such horrible things, as even to awaken my own fears. Generally however, I laughed heartily at the idea of ghosts and said I should like to see one.'

"'Oh don't say so,' said Amy, one night. 'What should we do if one should appear?'

"'I do wish one would,' returned I, 'how you would run.'

"Just then I heard a terrible crash, as if all the crockery and tinware upon the kitchen dressers had tumbled down.

"'What can that be,' I cried in alarm.

"'What?' asked my brother, very quietly.

"'Are you deaf?' I retorted. 'Don't you hear that dreadful noise? There it is again. Oh, what shall I do?'

"It was no wonder I was frightened for there sat my brother and sister as if they heard nothing, while every moment the noise grew louder. I had always thought myself a very brave girl before, but I shook with alarm at these unearthly sounds, and shrieked with terror when the door opened, and a terrible figure surrounded by blue flame entered the room. I pointed at it in speechless horror. It towered nearly to the ceiling and looked down upon me with eyes that glowed like coals. It held in its hand a whip made of snakes with which it menaced me. For a few seconds I could neither move nor speak, while my brother and sister laughed and talked as if nothing unusual was going on. I was convinced that this revelation from the spirit world was made to me alone, and I was overwhelmed by the fear that I was to be carried away bodily, to answer before the ghosts I had derided. The monster advanced toward me. With a shriek I bade it begone! it laid its death cold hand upon me and—

"'Oh, Miss Carry, don't tell any more.'

"'Oh, it was so horrible!' cried Aggie,

clasping Guy's arm lightly. "Oh dear, dear, didn't you die with fright?"

"It appears not," returned Miss Graham, laughing, "but I do not know but I should have done so, had not my brother James rushed into the room, caught hold of the supposed ghost and cried, 'there there, that will do Tom! Don't you see the poor child is nearly frightened to death.'

"So it wasn't a real ghost after all," exclaimed Aggie, in a tone of mingled disappointment and relief.

"No, it was not a real ghost after all, but only a very good sham one, that was made up by my brother and cousin to frighten me out of my propensity of frightening others, and you may be sure it did so. I didn't think I ever afterwards told a ghost story of which I could not as readily give an explanation as of this."

"But you frightened me though," said Aggie, drawing a long breath.

"But you are not frightened now, darling?"

"Why of course not Miss Carrie."

"But do you know I think I would rather hear that pretty little story about the 'Christ-child,' that you told us a few evenings ago, or one of those little poems of which you know so many."

"I do not think I can remember any tonight," said Miss Carrie, "but perhaps Amy can."

"Please try dear Miss Amy," cried Aggie running to her, "Mr. Graham, and Miss Carrie have both told us a story, and now if you will repeat some pretty poetry it will be so nice."

Miss Amy laughed pleasantly, and lifted Aggie on her lap. "My pet," she said, "yesterday I heard you ask your mother what she thought the prettiest thing in the world."

"Oh, yes," cried Aggie, "and she couldn't decide. What do you think the prettiest Miss Amy? But then perhaps you are like mamma, you think there are, so many beautiful things in the world that you can't choose between them.

"Yes," said Miss Amy sweetly though gravely, I have decided. "Now listen to me a few minutes and you shall know what is to me

FAIREST AND BEST:"

"There came a child to my side one day,
   And lightly she said with a laugh of mirth,
'Tell me of all things, now I pray,
   Which is the fairest to you upon earth?

"'Is it the rose, with its breath of balm?
   Is it the gem of the diamond mine?
Is it the shell, with its sea-song calm?
   Or the pearl, that low in the deep doth shine?'

"I answered her, 'Though the rose is fair,
    Though the diamond gleams like a lesser sun;
Oh, ne'er can *they*, e'en in thought compare,
    With my chosen beauty, my purest one.

"'For mine, far sweeter than rose doth bloom,
    In our world of sorrow, of woe, and care;
E'en light of the diamond seemeth gloom,
    To that halo divine that shineth where;

"'My fairest thing upon all the earth,
    A *little child* kneeleth down to pray,
And sweeter than sound of ocean's mirth
    Are the heav'nly words, she doth meekly say.

"Yes, as I look on a kneeling child,
    Of those I think, whom our Saviour blest,
And I know of all things fair and mild,
    The pure, young heart of a child is best.'"

Little Aggie remained perfectly still for some moments after Miss Amy had finished. At last she lifted up her face, and kissed the young lady sweetly, and whispered, "Dear Miss Amy I will try to remember that. I am sure Mamma thinks the same as you do. Thank you for telling me. Good-night my dear Miss. Amy. Good-night Miss Carrie, and Mr. Graham. We have had such a nice time haven't we Guy. Now we will go home,"

"Good-night, and good-night Mr. Graham, and Miss Carrie. Come, Guy, let us go home."

So Guy arose and led the little girl toward the wagon she called "home," for to her little affectionate heart any where was home where her parents stayed. They were walking slowly past the baggage wagons when to his surprise, and affright Guy saw a puff of smoke, issue from the back part of the one in which he usually slept. He instantly remembered the powder, and with a cry dashed toward it, bidding Aggie run as far as possible from the danger. There was no water near, but he caught up a bag of flour, sprang into the wagon and dashed it upon the flames, then another, and another. Meanwhile his cries had brought every one to the spot, James Graham brought a pail of water and threw upon the already smothered flames, and immediately a great sputtering, and kicking was heard, and George Harwood sat up sleepily and demanded what they were pitching into him for.

"Get up," said his father who was looking very pale and agitated, "Get up and thank this brave boy for having saved your life. If it had not been for him this powder would have exploded, and launched you, and we know not how many others into Eternity."

George saw how great his danger had been, and with shame owned that he had brought it upon himself, by dropping fire from a pipe which he was endeavoring to learn to smoke, in express disobedience of his father's commands.

He turned around to thank Guy for having risked his own life to save his, for that he had undoubtedly done by springing into the burning wagon, but found that like a true hero, he had gone to perform another duty, waiting neither for thanks or praises. But he got both, for as he lifted little Aggie into her mother's wagon, she kissed him and whispered "You good, brave boy, I am going to ask God to bless you all your life."

CHAPTER X.

"Well now, George," said Aggie the next morning, as they stood near the partially burned wagon and watched Mr. Harwood and his young men, as they hastily endeavored to repair the damage that had been done, "I should think you never would smoke again in your life."

"I didn't smoke last night," retorted George, "I only tried to, and to try to smoke and to do it are two very different things, I can tell you," and George grimaced most comically at the remembrance of some very extraordinary sensations he had experienced, both before and after the fire.

"If you don't believe me you can try it," he added, as Aggie looked at him thoughtfully.

"I wasn't thinking of what you were saying," she replied, "but of what a horrible death Guy saved you from."

"That's a fact," returned George, with much seriousness. "Guy ain't a bad sort after all!"

"Not a bit of a Guy Fawkes about him," commented Gus. "He don't believe in blowing up folks with gunpowder."

"Nor with words either," interrupted Aggie, "but who was Guy Fawkes, Gus?"

"Oh, a man put a lot of gunpowder in the cellar of the English House of Congress."

"Of Parliament," corrected George.

"Of Parliament, then, it means all the same thing, and he intended when the

King and all the members of Parliament were in the house to set fire to the powder and blow them all up. But they found out the plot just in time, and Guy was hung up, or had his head chopped of, I forget which."

"Good for him," said George. "Hullo, here comes Guy, looking really frightened for once in his life! What is the matter, Guy?"

But Guy made him no answer, but hurried on to Mr. Harwood and whispered a few words in his ear.

"You don't say so!" he ejaculated with a startled look. "Whereabouts are they?"

"Back of the camp, sir. Mr. Graham says he thinks they are after the cattle and horses. But they are to far off for us to see them plainly, and it was some time before I could make Mr. Graham believe they were Indians at all."

"Indians!" exclaimed George and Gus, turning pale, and with out more ado, rushing from the spot, not only as they said "to tell mother," but to gain a place of safety.

"Take Aggie to the wagon," said Mr. Harwood hastily, though he could not help smiling at the precipitate flight of his boys. "Be as quick as you can, and bring me my telescope."

Guy did as he was bidden, but although so quickly that he did not even take time to say a few words of encouragement to Aggie. He found the telescope was little needed when he gave it into Mr. Harwood's hands. The Indians had drawn so close that their movements could be perfectly seen.

"At least thirty young braves!" said Mr. Harwood anxiously. "A party of horse thieves no doubt! We shall have trouble!"

"And all on account of this unfortunate delay!" exclaimed Mr. Graham. "We should have been on our way three hours ago, but for your son's carelessness."

"That is very true. Yet we should scarcely have escaped the quick eyes of these wild savages."

"We will try to save the oxen and horses from their hands at least!" cried a young man, turning to a group who had hastily armed themselves.

In an incredible short space of time they had made a circle of the wagons, and within this barricade they placed the cattle, and stationed themselves at regular distances without the wagons. Mr. Harwood and Mr. Graham stood beside the wagon in which all the ladies had congregated, and with quiet, though great anxiety, waited for the attack to be commenced. They had no idea that it could be avoided for all Mr. Harwood's signals, during the formation of the barricade had been totally disregarded, and the savages in all the hideousness of paint and warlike decorations were riding rapidly around the camp in a gradually decreasing circle.

"Guy, my boy, you had better go into our wagon," said Mr. Harwood, as Guy, with a favorite dog at his side, drew near to him. Guy looked him doubtfully a moment, and with visible reluctance proceeded to obey the direction which had been given him. Suddenly, however, he turned back and with an appealing look at Mr. Harwood said:

"I wish you would give me a gun, sir, and let me stay here."

"Do as you please," cried Mr. Harwood hastily, and Guy rushed to a wagon for the desired weapon, and back again to his place.

Just then the Indians made a feint of going away. They retired slowly a little way, then suddenly wheeled, and galloped back towards the camp, discharging a volley of arrows as they came.

Fortunately they injured no one, but the second fire was not so harmless, and was returned steadily by Mr. Harwood and his men from their rifles. But the Indians were too far off, and changed their positions too often to be affected by it.

The firing continued in this manner for fifteen minutes or more. Two of Mr Harwood's men were seriously wounded, and obliged to retire to the wagons, and the others were eagerly speaking of dividing into two parties, one of which was to remain to guard the camp, while the other sallied out to drive off the Indians. It seemed a mad undertaking, as Mr. Harwood said, to divide so small a force, and they were spared the necessity of doing so by the savages themselves, who enraged at the death of one of their number, and confident of success, rode boldly up to the very sides of the wagons, and with showers of arrows, and brandishing their war-clubs, uttering at the same time the most dreadful yells, endeavored to overcome the white men and gain possession of the animals, that snorting and plunging with terror at the unusual rounds of shouting and firing were striving vainly to break their bounds. Terrible was the struggle that ensued. For a few minutes the shrieks of the women and children, the shouts of the white men, the yells of the Indians, the reports of fire-arms, and the indescribable noises made by the frightened animals filled the air.

Guy was almost stunned with the noise and bewildered by the confusion that prevailed. He never thought of firing his gun, and had no idea which party had the advantage, he, in fact, felt perfectly overwhelmed, not with fear, but horror, and quite regardless of his danger, remained an inactive spectator of the scene, until he beheld Mr. Harwood struggling violently with an Indian who had thrown himself from his horse in the excitement of the fight.

Mr. Harwood was himself a muscular man, and the struggle between the two was terrible to witness. For a minute neither seemed to have the advantage, then the strong Indian got his arm across Mr. Harwood's breast and held him back, he raised his right hand in which glittered a long knife already stained with blood. Some unusual sound for a moment attracted the savage's attention, he glanced around. Guy seized the opportunity, raised his gun and fired.

He was not knocked over by the shock, but the Indian was. Down he went, and Mr. Harwood with him, but only to remain there a moment. He sprang up and echoed the shout of triumph which was heard from the other side of the camp.

The fight was ended; the Indians defeated, away they sped with lightning speed, bearing their wounded, among which was Mr. Harwood's special adversary, with them, and leaving their dead upon the ground.

Of these there were two. But little notice was taken of them at first, for the members of the train were too busy attending to the wounded, and examining their own hurts, to think of Indians, unless it was to look occasionally to satisfy themselves that they were really gone, and that there was no farther trouble to be apprehended from them.

"I wonder who it was that knocked that great fellow over that was holding me down," said Mr. Harwood, after he had embraced his family, and assured them that he was very little hurt. "I wish I knew who it was, I have somebody to thank for saving my life."

"Here is the fellow!" cried Gus, catching Guy as he was about to jump from the wagon. He has got one of your guns, too, and it was only a little while ago you told him not to touch them."

"Guy!" exclaimed Mr. Harwood, "can it be possible that you fired that well-directed shot?"

"I couldn't help it, sir, the ball seemed to know just where to go, and the gun to shoot of itself," returned Guy, with a slight laugh—a vain attempt to hide his emotion.

Mr. Harwood made no effort to conceal

his, and catching him in his arms embraced him warmly, as he exclaimed! "My dear boy, have I then my own life to thank you for, as well as that of my son? How shall I be able to repay you?"

"Don't say any more," entreated Guy, who was being nearly suffocated by his mother, Mr. Harwood and the children, who were pulling him hither and thither to their heart's content.

"Why didn't you shoot his head right off?" ask George, when the commotion had slightly subsided. "I would if I had had a gun, and been in your place."

"But you weren't at all likely to be in his place or any other where arrows were flying," interrupted Gus, with a laugh, which quickly subsided into a smothered titter as George looked at him, with the remark: "You had better mind your bones."

"I intend to," said Gus, coolly, "but you needn't glare at me so. You're not a Gorgon, I guess, and can't turn me into stone by a look."

"I am very glad Guy didn't knock the Indian's head right off," interposed Aggie, anxious to prevent a quarrel between the two boys.

"Aren't you glad of it, Guy, you wouldn't have liked to have killed him dead, would you?"

"Oh no!" returned Guy, laughing. "It answered my purpose just to kill him a little. Indeed," he added, turning pale at the thought, "I hope the poor man will not die."

"Don't trouble yourself about that," said Mr. Harwood, taking in his hand the gun which Guy had still retained, but then offered him, "you nobly did your duty, my boy, and though we will hope that the man will recover, we will not worry, because we cannot learn whether he does or not."

"I say, the men are harnessing the teams," exclaimed George. "Let us go and pick up some of the arrows the Indians threw around so plentifully."

"Yes," answered Guy, "and I'll bring you one, Aggie."

"Stay," said Mr. Harwood, "Here, Guy, is a more fitting weapon for you. Take this gun, and though I hope you may never again be obliged to use it against a fellow-creature, I hope your shots will always be as well directed as that of to-day."

"Whew!" ejaculated George, "don't I wish I had knocked that fellow over to-day! Guy, why don't you say thank you?"

"He's like the little boy that would not say 'thank you,' for a new jack-knife," laughed Gus, "he'd rather use the old 'un fust."

In truth, Guy was so delighted with Mr. Harwood's words, and the gift that accompanied them, that he knew not what to say. To possess a gun, had long been his highest and most secret ambition, and to have one, really his own, in his hands, seemed, as he afterwards said, "far too good to be true."

"Never mind the thanks," exclaimed Mr. Harwood, as Guy vainly tried to utter something, "we understand each other, though my debt is not paid yet. You can go now and look for arrows, if you like."

But Guy thought but little of arrows, or even of his gun, for some minutes after he left the wagon, for just then four of the mules, who had not recovered from their fright, broke away from the men who were trying to quiet them, and galloped across the plains in the opposite direction to that the Indians had taken. Two young men immediately mounted the swiftest horses in the train and set off in pursuit, and a fine chase they had. Over an hour passed before they brought the refractory animals back, and an exciting time the boys had watching the race, and shouting and hurrahing when the foaming, panting creatures rushed into the camp, followed by their almost breathless pursuers.

"But this isn't finding arrows!" said Guy, at last, suddenly remembering Aggie, and the promise he had made her. And, after the train was in motion, he found two beautiful arrows, and took them to her. She accepted them with delight, telling Guy she would keep them all her life, in remembrance of that eventful day. "And so you see," she added, addressing in fancy the cross old chief that had frightened her so terribly, "I have got one of your Indian arrows, after all, and I'll keep it too. My good Guy has got a gun now, and that's more than you have, and he knows how to use it, that's more than you will ever do."

CHAPTER XI.

Two weeks after the fight with the Indians, Guy was galloping across the gently rising hills, that denoted their approach to the Rocky Mountains, in quest of game. This was the first time he had had an opportunity offered him to try his gun, as they had seen no living creature upon the desert of alkali which they had occupied more than a week in crossing, and but few among the prickly pears and sage-brush that succeeded the poisonous salts. Of the effects of the latter, each member of the party had had some experience, and all, for weeks after, complained of sore lips, chapped hands, and other pains of a like nature.

Guy was greatly troubled to find that little Aggie and his mother were the greatest sufferers. Indeed, the latter became so very ill that, for two or three days, Guy feared he should soon be motherless. Never had his heart been so heavy as during that time. It was a good thing for him that he was obliged to work additionally hard, else he might also have fallen ill from excessive grief. But, as it was, he had no time to give way to his feeling: there was his mother's duties and his own, to be performed by his hands alone; little Aggie to be amused, and his mother often to be cheered by some gay word, when he usually felt much more like uttering sad ones.

I have mentioned before that Mrs. Loring, though a very good woman, was often inclined to look on the dark side of things, and so it sometimes happened that she led Guy to do the same, and he certainly did so steadily enough during the days his mother lay seriously ill, while he turned to the bright side instantly when she pronounced herself better, though he did not for a moment neglect to pay her the same attention as before.

One morning, when she, for the first time, gathered strength and energy enough to sit up, Mr. Harwood entered the wagon, and laughingly told her that as she was so well, he should not let her have Guy to herself any longer, but should take him with them to hunt some deer that were feeding on the hills some distance away. Guy looked at his mother and hesitated, for though he desired, above all things, to take part in a deer hunt, he did not like to leave his sick mother, until she said: "Go, my child, you are looking pale and thin already, the excitement will do you good.

It would never do for you to get sick, you know." And that was how Guy Loring happened to be galloping across the hills with Mr. Harwood and Mr. Graham, while George and Gus remained at the camp, enviously watching him. By some skillful manœuvering, they managed to approach within gun-shot of the deer, of which there were five or six, brousing quietly. Guy was very much excited, and would have fired upon them had not Mr. Harwood told him not to do so until the last.

Slowly, and with as much patience as they could command, they drew nearer and nearer the deer. Mr. Graham and Mr. Harwood raised their rifles to fire, when suddenly the whole herd of deer threw their heads in the air, looked around wildly, and bounded away with the speed of the wind.

" What in the world could have startled

them so?" exclaimed the gentlemen in surprise.

Guy looked around in perfect dismay at having lost the chance of firing at a deer, and quickly exclaimed: "Oh, how provoking, it is the cattle. They have let the cattle loose."

Mr. Graham uttered an exclamation of delight, "Was there ever such good luck before?" he cried, "Those are buffaloes! I had no idea we should find them here so early. Gallop back to the camp, Guy, and tell the Fraziers! Hurrah!"

Scarcely less excited than Mr. Graham, Guy made a wide circuit of the spot where the herd of buffaloes, from twenty to thirty in number, were feeding, and galloped to the camp, where he found five or six young men, already armed and mounted for the chase. They hastily advised Guy to remain in camp, but as he had received no direction to do so from Mr. Harwood, he followed his inclinations, and returned with the young men to the spot where Mr. Graham and Mr. Harwood were anxiously awaiting them.

All this time the buffaloes continued to feed without taking the least notice of the hunters. These after a short consultation, began to ride gently towards them. The animals remained so quiet that Guy had an opportunity to look at them carefully. He was surprised to find that they were *not* as large as elephants, but on the contrary about the size of a cow, which animal they closely resembled in the shape of their bodies, and limbs; but their hair, instead of being of the same length all over their body, grew in shaggy tufts upon the back and sides, and lengthened into a sweeping mane upon the neck. This adornment took from them the peaceful expression of the majority of our domestic cattle, and gave them instead the terrible one of the untamed lion. This effect was increased by the wild glare of their eyes. Guy did not at first notice their horns, which were small, and almost imbedded in their thick, woolly hair, but it did not need a second look to assure him that they could do a great deal of harm, if once called into service. The hunters approached the buffaloes in a semi-circle, Guy occupied a place near the circle by the side of Mr. Harwood, who unwilling to disappoint him by sending him back to the camp, had permitted him to stay. The whole party got within a hundred feet of the buffaloes before they were even discovered. Then an immense fellow who seemed the leader of the herd, began to bellow, and tear up the earth with his hoofs, and in a moment, the whole herd were coursing over the prairie at a pace, which Guy, when looking at their heavy bodies, had never imagined them capable of.

"After them!" shouted Mr. Graham, and instantly the hunters spurred on their horses many of which were used to the sport, and in a few minutes Guy, who was poorly mounted was left some distance in the rear, while the foremost of the horsemen were at the very heels of the flying herd. The dust of the prairie began to rise from beneath their hoofs in clouds, through which Guy could indistinctly see the buffaloes dashing forward, one turning occasionally upon some audacious man who had fired upon him, who would then wheel his horse quickly and escape from the reach of the infuriated animal, which would continue its flight or fall to the earth, with a terrible bellow.

Guy had witnessed three or four such

falls, and in his excitement scarcely knowing what he did, went up to the foaming animal intending to put it out of its misery by a shot from his gun, when, suddenly, it rose to its feet, staggered forward, and ere Guy could wheel his frightened horse, plunged his horns into his breast, and buffalo, horse and rider rolled upon the plain together.

Then succeeded a horrible moment, in which Guy felt himself crushed by his plunging horse, and heard the cries of the men, the bellowing of the wounded buffalo, the thunderlike noise of the retreating herd, and the sharp crack of half a dozen rifles. Then he felt himself lifted from the ground by Mr. Graham and Mr. Harwood, who exclaimed that it was a miracle that he was alive, and asked him if he wasn't killed, and then shouted out for somebody to go in pursuit of the horse, which was galloping away in the opposite direction to the buffaloes, which were suffered to depart without any further attempt being made to slaughter them.

CHAPTER XII.

Guy was surprised and delighted to find that his fool-hardy escapade had brought upon him no injury except a few bruises, which, however, did not prevent him from assisting the men to take into camp the carcasses of the three buffaloes they had slain.

That proved a busy afternoon in the camp. The buffaloes were skinned, and their shaggy hides hung up in the sun to dry. Then the choicest parts of the bodies were cut up and salted, and the rest left to the hungry wolves, who are the natural enemies of the buffalo—one of which, when wounded, they will often follow, and harrass to death.

And what a splendid supper of buffalo steak they had. Guy fancied he never had tasted anything so delicious, though George, in his usual contradictory mood, declared he thought beef much nicer. But as no one paid any attention to him, his opinion had not much effect, and no one enjoyed the supper the less for it.

As only a slight sketch of Guy's wonderful escape had been given by Harwood upon his return to camp, the children were anxious to hear a full account of it, and as soon as the dishes were washed, the fuel for the night brought in and Guy was at liberty to take his usual seat by the fire, they called upon him to tell them all about it. He did so in as few words as possible, for he felt as much ashamed of his discomfiture as an old hunter might have been likely to do.

Aggie looked very serious after hearing

the account of her favorite's danger. George laughed as he thought of the figure Guy must have cut when pitched from his horse over the back of the buffalo; and Gus with great earnestness asked him what he thought of at the time it all happened.

"I saw and heard too much to think of anything," replied Guy, quite unable to repress a laugh at Gus' question and eager look, "the first thing I thought of when Mr. Graham took me from the ground was to clear the sand from my nose, eyes, and mouth. If you had seen me you would have fancied I had been burrowing in the dirt for a twelve month. After that I was very thankful that I escaped so well, and on the way home I recalled to mind almost everything I had ever read about buffaloes, and among other things a mode in which the Indians hunt them, and which is described in the adventures of Lewis and Clarke."

"Who were Lewis and Clarke?" asked Gus.

"Two men, who in the days of Washington and Jefferson, and chiefly by the aid of the latter, headed a party of men, who were the first to explore Oregon, and discover the rise of the Columbia and Missouri Rivers."

"What fun they must have had," exclaimed George, "among the Indians that had never seen a white man before."

"They were so constantly surrounded by dangers," said Guy, "that I guess they found the *fun* rather scarce. But they had a great many exciting adventures among the Indians, and learned many of their strange habits."

"Well, you were going to tell us about

a way they had of hunting buffaloes," interrupted Gus. "How was it?"

"Well, first they would find, either by accident or after a search, a herd of buffaloes, grazing on a plateau, perhaps three or four hundred feet above the river, for such are very often found a mile or more in length along the Columbia or Missouri Rivers, which abruptly terminate, forming a precipice so perfectly perpendicular that neither man or beast can gain a foothold on their sides.

"Toward this precipice a young warrior wrapped in a buffalo robe, and crowned with the head and horns, decoys the game, while the others chase them forward, riding their swiftest horses, bearing their best arms, and uttering their wildest shouts. The whole herd maddened by the hunters, will usually follow the decoy—their fancied leader—when suddenly he will hide beneath some cliff, the buffaloes will rush on, seeing no danger ahead, or unable to check their headlong career, and thus very often a hundred or more will spring over the precipice, and be dashed to pieces on the rocks below."

"Good!" cried George, excitedly.

"And just think then what a good time the Indians have picking up the pieces," commented Gus, I'd like to see them do it. Just think of two or three hundred Indians all at work together, jerking the meat, and shouting and dancing."

"Ah, yes. That's all very well!" said Aggie, thoughtfully. But I wouldn't like so much to be the decoy. Suppose he couldn't hide in time."

"Sometimes he can't," said Guy, "and in that case he is trodden under foot by the herd, or carried with them over the precipice. I am like you, Aggie, I shouldn't like to be the decoy. It is bad enough to face one buffalo, and I have no wish to try a hundred."

"Oh, dear!" exclaimed Aggie, "I should die with fright if I were to meet even one."

"Oh! That's because you are nothing but a girl—but boys—!". George left his sentence unfinished, for of late he had become very careful of boasting before Guy, whom he knew was too well acquainted with him to be deceived by empty words.

"Girls, or no girls!" exclaimed Aggie, a little angrily, "I learned those verses mamma gave us, to-day, while you don't know them at all!"

"Verses are only made for girls!" answered George, contemptuously.

"And for some boys," said Guy, "I for one like to hear them. What are yours about Aggie?"

"Listen! They are about

'THE CHILDREN IN THE SKY.'

"Little Allie, tired with roaming,
   Fell asleep one summer day;
In the soft, and mellow gloaming,
   That the fairies haunt, they say.
And, into her dream, there came then
   Fays, or Angels pure and fair,
Filling all the lonesome glen
   With sweet music, rich and rare.

"'Child!' they said, as slow around her
   One by one they floated on,
'Look into the clearer ether,
   Close beside the setting sun!'
Then she looked, and lo! the cloudlets
   Parted back and showed her there,
Myriad angels, sinless spirits
   Sporting in a garden fair.

"Sporting, smiling, fondly twining,
   Round each other snow white arms;
While a halo o'er them shining,
   Saved them from the night's alarms.
Loud they sung in notes of gladness,
   Ever o'er the sweet refrain;
'Jesus loves us! we shall never
   Lose His tender care again.''

"'Here the flow'rets bloom forever;
  Here the sun of God doth shine;
Here doth flow the crystal river,
  Giving all a life divine!'
Then the peerless vision faded,
  And the fairies stole away;
All the dell with gloom was shaded,
  Darkness 'round sweet Allie lay.

"Then she woke from out her slumber,
  And she said—within her heart—
'Shall I join that happy number?
  In their joyous song take part?'
Then she prayed that God would lead her
  In the path to heaven above,
And that she might dwell forever
  Blessed by Christ's redeeming love.

"And before the year was over,
  God in love gave back reply,—
For He led the little rover,
  To the children in the sky."

"That is a sweet little tale," said Guy, when Aggie had finished, "But it is almost a pity such a good little girl should die."

"But the good little girls, in stories, always do die!" exclaimed George, "And that is why I don't like to hear about them. That's the reason, too, that I tease our Aggie so, I want to get her into a passion so she won't get too good and be spirited out of the world right away."

They all laughed at this ingenious defense; and then as Guy declared himself very tired, and quite stiff and sore from the number of bruises upon his body, they soon separated for the night, and ere long all was still about the camp, except the fires that flickered and blazed, as if in derision of the calm night, and its heavy-eyed attendant—Sleep.

CHAPTER XIV.

The following Saturday night found the party encamped in the very bosom of the mountains, in one of the most lovely nooks upon the surface of the earth. As they looked around upon the verdant dell, and upon the snow-capped mountains that arose in the distance, all the arid plain they had passed,—the desert of alkali, and the hills .of sand—seemed like a dream, so great was the contrast between them and Virginia Dale. Even George was enraptured, and when the children as usual gathered at evening around the fire, he declared that he would go no father but turn hermit, and hunt and fish for a living, in that lovely spot.

"I wish I could stay with you," said Aggie, "but I should'nt like to leave papa and mamma. But only look at the moon rising above that snowy peak; isn't it perfectly lovely?"

"Watching the moon is all very well?" exclamed Gus, "but I would much rather hear a good story. This is the very night for a story, and a sentimental one at that. Guy get your thinking-cap on, that's a good fellow!"

"Oh yes, do!" assented Aggie.

"I have had it tightly drawn over my ears the whole time I have been sitting here," answered Guy laughing, "and the result is that I have been thinking of a story the Indians tell about the first snow storm."

"Oh yes! put it all off on the Indians!" cried Gus, "we all know what that means!"

"Well, what do they say?" asked George,

"that they thought it was salt, and put it into their soup, and were surprised to find that it made it watery—and nothing more?"

"Now don't tease Guy," interrupted Aggie, "I want to know what the Indians really did say, and where the first fall of snow really was."

"According to my authority," answered Guy, gravely, "it took place among these very mountains. Years, years ago, so many years that all rememberance of the time is now lost, and only vague reports of it remain, the snowy mountains we now see were covered with verdure, even more luxuriant than that which makes this vale so beautiful. The long leaves, and the shining silk of the corn waved in the breeze that softly played about the lofty summits, lovely flowers opened, and rich fruits ripened in the warm sunshine that ever fell upon them. The bounding deer came to the very doors of the wigwams that were so thickly placed that they seemed to form a vast city, and the very trout in the sparkling streams leaped into the hands of the happy people that inhabited this earthly paradise!"

"Gracious, what a saving of fishing-tackle!" ejaculated George.

Guy took no notice of this irreverent remark, but continued:

"On the very summit of yonder peak, which seems to rise at least a thousand feet above its neighbors, and where the sun shone the warmest, the grains and fruits were most luxuriant, and the deer larger and tamer than in any other place, lived an old man, the chief of all the tribes that lived between the mountains and the great ocean in the far west. The oldest men among the Indians could not remember when he was young, and their great-grandfathers had told them that he was old when they were children. His beard was like silver, and his face bore the marks of that wisdom which can only come with age, yet his form was not bent, and his eyes were as strong as the eagle's, that soars up and looks in the face of the sun."

"Wonderful man!" said Gus.

"He was indeed wonderful, and the wisest man upon the earth; he knew all secrets of the land, and sea, and air, and from them he had gained the elixir that still kept the blood warm in his veins after the lapse of centuries, but he could not get from them contentment,—his soul at last wearied of the habit of clay it had worn so long, and he began a search for one worthy to be the inheritor of his wisdom, and the successor of his power, that he might lie down and be at rest.

"He found one at length, but not among the young men of his tribe, among whom he sought long and patiently. The strength of mind, the purity of soul he desired, were found only in the person of a lovely girl, the daughter of one of the bravest warriors of the mountains. To her he gave the elixir of life, and instructed her in all the secrets he had gained. Lastly, he took off the robe he wore, and putting it upon her, led her out of the wigwam and declared her a priestess before all the people. Soon after the great magician became a decrepit old man, the weight of his years came upon him and he died, and his body was laid upon a burning pile and consumed to ashes, while all the people mourned around it. Then the priestess went to her wigwam on the high mountains and sat down and thought of the last words the dead man had said to her, 'Beware of him who reigneth at the northernmost part of the earth, for if thou showest weakness or any human passion he will have dominion over thee and all thy people.' But years passed on and no human feeling agitated her. She lived alone communing with spirits, and at sundry times appearing among the people to astonish them by her wisdom which as years advanced, become a thousand times more potent than had been that of the old magician. And as her wisdom increased so also did her beauty. Spirits came and took the ebony from her hair, and covered it with gold; they brought blue from the skies and prisoned it in her eyes; the white stars laid their light upon her face, and sunbeams rendered her smile so warm and tender that it gladdened all upon whom it fell.

"As I have said, she was troubled by no human feeling; but alas! she inspired what she did not feel, for all the young braves worshipped her, not only as a priestess, but as a peerless maiden, and all their awe could not destroy their love. As she knew every thing, she was of course aware of their silent devotion, but she laughed in the solitude of her wigwam, and sang:

'Alstarnah must no passion own,
That mortal e'er before hath known.'

"And this she would sing over and over to herself, that she might keep the words of the magician in mind. But after the lapse of many years, she one day ceased to sing, for Alstarnah felt the most powerful of all human passions—she loved."

"I'm glad of that!" ejaculated Gus, "just paid her out for keeping up that montonous drone so long."

"Oh! don't interrupt!" cried Aggie, impatiently, "who did she love, Guy?"

"The young chief, Gervassen, who had come many thousand miles from the burning plains of the far south, to behold the renowned priestess of the mountains. As Alstarnah excelled all women in beauty and wisdom, so did he all men in beauty and strength. He was as tall and slender as the mountain pine, and his face was as fair to look upon as the great star that hung above the North King's palace. He came to the mountains with great pomp, for a thousand of his enemies pursued him, and he slew them all with the masses of rock that he hurled down upon them. See, there they lie now like mighty castles in ruins.

"When the priestess, Alstarnah, saw this man she thought no more of the magician's words or of her own power, but gloried in the beauty that had been given her, and said, 'He will surely love me, for there is not upon all the earth a woman as fair.'

'And her words were true, Gervassen did love her, and more bold than all the rest, entreated her to be his wife. With great joy she placed her hand in his, but at the moment she was about to speak, she felt an icy wind blow over her and a voice exclaim: 'Beware of the King of the North! Pity thy people!'

"She fled to her wigwam in terror, and for days refused to admit the chieftain, who stood without pleading for an answer but at length she ventured to glance at him through a tiny hole in the buffalo hide that formed the walls of her tent, and in an instant all her love for her people and all fear of the warning voice vanished, and she promised to be Gervassen's bride.

"Again came the icy wind and the voice,

but so infatuated was she that they failed to turn her from her purpose, although her lover asked the meaning of them. She trembled as she told him that years before there had been a tremendous battle waged between the King of the North and the forces of the great magician. That the latter had finally triumphed, after a terrible struggle, and after yielding one important point to his enemy, which was, that if the magician or any of his successors yielded to human passion, the help of the spirits should be withdrawn from them, and their dominion and people left to the power of the terrible North King.

"'It cannot be that he exists,' returned the warrior, 'else he would have endeavored to enter the land over which my tribe is scattered, and never, never has one of his subjects been seen or heard of upon it.'

"In spite of all her wisdom, this reasoning of Gervassen convinced Alstarnah, who soon after stood up before all the people and bade them farewell, saying that she was going to dwell in the wigwam of the mighty chieftain, Gervassen.

"Then she took her lover's hand and began the descent of the charmed mountain, followed by all her people, who were weeping and wailing, and entreating that she would come back to them. But still she went on, but only slowly, because of the great press of people around her; and suddenly an icy wind passed over them, and all fell to the earth shivering and terror-stricken, for they had never felt cold before, and they looked up to the mountain, and lo! upon the very summit, at the door of the deserted wigwam, stood a terrible figure, clothed in white, and having a face as white as his robes, and his hair was like the long crystals that hang from the roofs of caves that the water goes through, and his eyes were like two great diamonds, white, yet blazing like the sun. Over his head he waved a sceptre, and as fast as he waved, great flakes of whiteness came out of the clouds and covered all the mountain tops, and came nearer and nearer to the frightened people.

"'It is the terrible North King,' they cried. 'See, he is throwing his arrows upon us.'

"'I will return,' cried Alstarnah, filled with remorse. 'I will return and save my people.'

"But once more she heard the voice as it wailed 'Too late! too late!' and the icy wind came and arrested her returning footsteps, for it chilled her to ice by the side of Gervassen, for whom she had dared so much. Then he and all the people were filled with still greater terror and turned to flee down the mountains, but the snow flakes—the deadly arrows of the North King, came faster and faster, falling before as well as behind them, clogging the feet and chilling the life-blood of the people Alstarnah had betrayed.

"First, Gervassen fell, almost at the side of Alstarnah: then, one by one, all the rest of the people sank down and were buried by the soft, white snow, until at last not one remained to tell of the verdure that once crowned the mountains where the North King still reigns, or of the people he slew with terrible arrows of snow, like those he still loves to throw in derision upon any daring traveler that attempts to invade his dominions."

"And that is the story of the first Snow Storm."

"I'll tell you what, Guy," commented

George, "You won't tell stories about facts, I know, but you make up for it when you have fancies to deal with."

Guy laughed, saying, "He supposed there was no harm in that."

And little Aggie said, as she bade him good-night, "I guess you will be forgiven even if there is, Guy. And I am sure I shall never look at these mountains or see snow again without thinking of your story."

CHAPTER XV.

For some time Aggie found no difficulty in keeping her word, for the train were obliged to pass over a part of the Rocky Mountains, and many a strange adventure they met upon the way. Those that had been over the route before said they got along remarkably well, while those to whom the experience was new, declared that with the breaking down of some wagons, the unloading of others, and letting them and goods they contained down the precipices by ropes, and the accidents attendant upon such work, they found the journey anything but delightful. The children enjoyed this part of the trip more than any other, for, with the exception of

Guy, they had no more work to do, and had much more to interest and amuse them.

But upon the whole they were rather glad when they got upon the level ground again, and especially so when they neared the shores of the great Salt Lake, and passed by the city that stands upon its shores.

Mr. Harwood had intended to visit it, and spend three or four days in looking about the city and endeavoring to learn something about the manners and customs of the people that inhabited it, but several of the party were anxious to reach their destination, and for that and many other reasons they passed the dwelling place of the Mormons by. Although the children were greatly disappointed at not being able to go into the city, they could not help speaking and thinking with delight of the beautiful country they had passed over to reach it.

"It seems to me," said Aggie one day when they stopped to rest, "that four seasons had wandered out of some years and lost themselves up among those mountains."

"You're crazy!" said George contemptuously."

"I think not," said Guy kindly, "but what could have put such a queer idea as that into your head, Aggie?"

"Why you know," she said, "the grass was fresh and green there as if it was spring time, and yet very often while you were gathering buttercups to make me a chain, George and Gus would be pelting you with snow-balls, while the summer sun was shining upon us all the day long."

"That's so," exclaimed George, "I should

never have thought of it again. It's the queerest place I ever saw in my life, except this very great valley which we are in now. Papa says it is over three hundred miles from the Rocky Mountains to the Sierra Nevadas, yet although we haven't been out of sight of the first for more than a week, we shall see the tops of the others in a few days, and then, hurrah! we've only to cross them and we shall be in California! Won't that be glorious?"

"Yes, I shall be glad," said Aggie, "for I was beginning to think as mamma said the other day, 'that we never should see a house again.' And won't you be glad, Guy, not to have to get up so early to make the fires in the morning, and to work so late at night, often after walking over the hot sands all day?"

"I don't know," said Guy rather sadly, "You have all been very kind to me here, and though I have often worked very hard, I guess it won't be all play for *me* in California."

Little Aggie often thought of these words of Guy in the days that followed, as they drew nearer and nearer their destination, and each member of the company spoke of his or her hopes or prospects. She noticed that upon that Guy, as well as his mother, was always silent, and many, many hours she sat in the wagon puzzling her little head as to what would become of their favorite.

She even spoke of it to Guy when they were alone together, but he seldom would say anything about it. He was not like some people that find comfort in talking over perplexing questions, and it certainly was a very perplexing question to him, how he was to support his mother in the strange country to which he had induced her to come, for though young, Guy was too wise to think that gold lay all over the land, and all that any one had to do was to stoop and pick it up, though many older than himself in the train still believed that old fable, which deceived many in the time of Cortez, over two hundred years before.

But although Guy was so uncertain as to what his fate would be in California, he soon became as anxious to reach it as the rest, for nothing for many weeks occurred to break the monotony of their journey, and the only excitement they had at all was in looking out for Indians, which were said to be very plenty upon their route, and in being constantly pleasurably disappointed in not coming upon any.

One day, indeed, they were greatly surprised by the descent of a terrific rain storm upon them, for they had never dreamed of encountering rain in that elevated region, where not even a drop of dew was found in the early morning. At the time it occurred a party from the train, among whom was Guy, were out hunting. They saw the black clouds rising above the mountains, but leisurely continued their way intent upon obtaining some game for supper, when, suddenly, a blast of wind swept down upon them, bringing with it torrents of water, as if, as Guy afterwards said, another deluge had come to sweep every living thing from the earth's surface.

For a moment the horses stood still as if stunned, and their riders bent low over the saddles, then, suddenly wheeling, the animals turned their heads away from the furious blast, and in that position waited for it to expend its fury. Neither whip nor spur would induce them to move, though Mr. Harwood used both freely, being anxious to gain the camp and satisfy himself of the safety of his family. The horses chose the best position, according to the instinct which had been given them to escape from danger, and they maintained it until the fury of the storm was spent, and then obediently carried their riders to the camp, where they found two or three of the lighter wagons blown over, and a number of articles scattered hither and thither. All the people however were safe though greatly frightened.

CHAPTER XVI.

As George said, the great rain storm seemed to have come expressly to wash all interest out of their journey, for from that day until their arrival within sight of Carson River, within the Territory of Nevada, where a part of the company were to part from the main body, they saw but little to interest them. True they had passed over a wonderful country, but the alkali plains seemed small in comparison to the desert, over which they had passed some weeks before, and all the grandeur of the Sierra Nevada Mountains could not awaken in them one iota of the enthusiasm with which they had greeted the first glimpse of the snow-capped summits of the Rocky

Mountains. In fact they were too weary of their long journey to look around them for enjoyment, but rather looked forward to it, when all deserts of alkali, of sand and sage-brush being past, they might by the rivers and in the peaceful vales of California find rest and plenty.

As I have said before, all in the company but Guy and his mother had something to look forward to. Many of the young men were going to the placer diggings or the deep mines, and spoke exultantly of the rich harvest they would surely glean. Mr. Graham had a quartz mill in a very fine situation, and he was going to take charge of it, and his sisters were to keep house for him, while Mr. Frazer and Mr. Harwood had decided to purchase farms and settle upon them.

The last night that all in the train were to encamp together, a large fire was built and all gathered around it to talk over their plans. Guy sat by Aggie's side and tried to talk to her, but he could not help listening to what was said, and that, with the knowledge that they were so near California—their journey's end,—made him feel so miserable that he walked away from the fire, and hid himself in a dark place, and cried as if his heart would break.

What was he to do when compelled to leave these friends? Almost penniless where was he in that new, unsettled country to find a home for his mother. For himself he could provide, but what should he do for his mother? He had heard that work, hard work, was plenty; but his mother could not do hard work; it had nearly killed her before, and doubtless there were few children to be taught. What could he do with her? Where should he leave her, while he went to try his fortune?

It never entered his head to ask any one to give her a home. He felt under unpayable obligations already to Mr. Harwood for bringing them so far upon their way, and treating them so kindly, therefore to ask him to do more, he thought would be the greatest presumption, so instead of asking help of any man, he asked it of God.

He was still sitting with his head bowed on his knees, and the tears streaming down his cheeks, most earnestly praying, when, suddenly, a flash from the light of a lantern passed over him, and a voice exclaimed: "why, here you are, I have been searching for you for ever so long."

It was one of the young men from St. Louis, with whom Guy had been on most excellent terms ever since they left W—.

"Yes, it is I," he returned, rather reluctantly, for he was ashamed that he should have found him crying. "What is the matter, John?" he presently added.

"The matter! why, don't you know we are to break up camp to-morrow, and one party go one way into California, and the other another! Now, which one are you going with, Guy?"

"I don't know," he said, with difficulty repressing a sob, "one part of California is the same to me as another. I have no friends there, and, oh dear, I very much fear I ought not to have come at all."

"Oh, don't say that," exclaimed John, cheerfully, "you just come along with me and my partners, we are going straight to the placer diggings, and we'll take care of you until you can do for yourself, which won't be long, you may be sure; I should'nt wonder if you're as rich as Rothschild in a few years."

Guy's eyes sparkled, but in a moment his countenance fell, and he faltered out,—

"But what is to become of mother,—I could'nt leave her alone in a strange country, her heart would break."

"Sure enough, I never thought of her, but something might be done, she would'nt break her heart, if she didn't starve."

"Ah, but she might do both!" exclaimed Guy. "Indeed, I cannot leave her. We must live and strive together, John. I thank you for your offer, but I can't leave my mother."

"You're a nobler fellow than the Spartan that let the wolf gnaw his vitals rather than cry out," replied the young man, "and though you won't join us, Guy, I don't doubt but you'll find good fortune somewhere."

"Thank you," said Guy, and comforted by the young man's kind offer, though he could not accept it, he walked back to the fire, where he found only the Grahams and the Harwoods.

"We have been talking about you, Guy," said Mr. Harwood. "Mr. Graham says he will give you a place in the mill if you will go with him."

"That I will, sir!" cried Guy, joyfully, his heart bounding, then falling like lead as he added, " but my mother?"

"I think she will consent," said Mr. Graham.

"Oh, sir, it was not of that I was thinking, it was of what would become of her. Oh, sir, she is poor and friendless, and I could'nt think of leaving her alone."

"I say then," said George, who had apparently been engaged in building castles in the air, or anything else rather than listening to the conversation, "I say, now that Guy isn't going with Mr. Graham, it's cold enough up there to kill his mother, make an icicle of her before Christmas, you know you said last night it was."

"Is that true, sir?" asked Guy, turning to Mr. Graham.

"Why, I can't say that your mother would be an icicle before Christmas," returned Mr. Graham, laughing, "but it certainly is far too cold and stormy there for a delicate woman."

"Ah, then, sir!" returned Guy, very sadly, "I cannot go with you, I cannot leave my mother."

"Hurrah!" cried George, turning a double somersault before the fire, and nearly into it.

"What's the matter?" asked Guy, in astonishment.

"Why, it means," said Mr. Harwood,

"that if you will not leave your mother, you must stay with us, as she has consented to do. Much as I disliked to part with you, who have been so invaluable to me on the way, I did not like to ask you to remain with us while others were ready to offer you, in mines and mills, so much better opportunities of gaining money than I can upon my little farm. There, for some time at least, there will be more work than money, I guess. So now, Guy, you know your mother will, at any rate, have a home; Mr. Graham will give you much higher wages than I can."

At that point, Aggie began to cry bitterly, saying, "Guy, you musn't go away! who should I have to tell me stories?"

"And, besides, my dog Jack can't smoke yet," interrupted Gus, "and you promised to teach him, and you've got to stay and do it."

"That's so," said George. "I expect I shall burn the house down trying to smoke, if you don't. You see I haven't forgotten how you threw that flour and water on me in the burning wagon, yet, and you have to stay and let me have satisfaction for that!"

"Yes, do stay," said Aggie, coaxingly.

"I intend to," cried Guy, bursting out into a loud laugh to prevent himself from crying with joy at his good fortune. "Hasn't it nearly broken my heart to think of leaving you, Aggie, and Mr. and Mrs. Harwood, and all the rest? Indeed, I would rather be with you all, if you were as poor as—as—"

"Job's turkey," suggested George.

"Well, yes, or as I am myself, than be a prince without you."

After which burst of eloquence Guy sat down, bringing a scream of dismay from

Aggie, upon whom he had inadvertently seated himself.

"Now that is all settled," said Mr. Harwood, dismissing the matter in his usual cool way, though one could see he was much gratified, "we will have prayers."

He arose and rung the large bell and all the company gathered around him, as they had often done upon the plains and the mountains, and listened to the word of God. Then he spoke to them of what had passed, and gave his best wishes to each. All were much affected at his kindly words, and by the short prayer that followed. There were few dry eyes there as those that were to leave on the morrow bade farewell, and it was with deep grief Guy parted with his many friends.

At daybreak next morning the final separation took place, a long train of waggons diverged to another path, leaving the families of Mr. Frazer and Mr. Harwood to take their way alone into California.

CHAPTER XVII.

A month later they were there, and not only there but settled upon fine farms adjoining each other. To be sure they had but very small dwellings to live in, but all were too much pleased with the green meadows, sloping down to the river's edge, and the beautiful forests that crowned the hills that lay in the background, to fret because the walls of their house were made of sun-dried mud instead of stone. They found too many things to be thankful for, to find time to complain of any, and although all things were very rough, and Mrs. Harwood and Mrs. Loring wondered a hundred times a day "what they should do," they finally decided, when everything in the little house was arranged to their satisfaction, that they should do very well indeed.

"Yes, very well," said Mrs. Loring, for although she called herself a servant, and was paid as such, she did not feel degraded by it, for she knew she was earning an honest living, and was respected as a friend by her employers, while Guy was looked upon almost as a son. He took the same place with the children as that held in their trip across the plains. He worked for their father, and for them, and very hard too, sometimes, but he was still their playfellow, George's guide, Gus' friend, little Aggie's comforter, and singer of songs, and teller of stories to all. As I have said, he worked hard, for even with a kind, indulgent master, like Mr. Harwood, much is thrown upon the hands of a willing boy, so Guy found there was still fires to light in the morning, water to fetch, wood to chop and carry, cows to milk, and the plough to be followed.

Sometimes he grew tired of the dull routine, and would wish himself at the diggings with the young men from St. Louis, and then with Mr. Graham, at the mill, but a glance at his mother, working over the hot stove, or washing at the spring, would render him content, for he would say, "She is happy with all her toil, while I am near, and shall I worry over a little extra work, when it keeps me with her?" And then away to his work he would go with renewed energy, and sometimes Mr. Harwood would give him a holiday which would quite revive his drooping spirits, and make him strong for weeks.

Oh, what holidays these were! Off all the children would go to the woods, that in the afternoon were full of sunshine, so warm, so beautiful; the grass would look like shaded velvet beneath them, and the leaves would glance and quiver as if they were fairies frolicking in their best clothes. And such woods as these were, in which to gather wild plums and nuts, and then to lie in the shade and tell fairy stories. "The very trees seem to say them over to us," said Aggie, the first day they spent in the woods together. "I am sure there must be something in all these sweet sounds we hear."

"Birds' songs," said George, contemptuously.

"No," said Aggie, "something more. Tell us what it is, Guy, you can always tell what the birds and animals say, you even told us what the prairie dogs said, you know."

Guy threw himself down on the green

grass beside a little brook, and listened, with his eyes fixed on the yellow sands of the little stream.

"The birds are telling me that there is gold in that sand," he said at length, "they tell me there is gold throughout all this wonderful country, in every rock and chasm, and there is one big fellow that is telling me how it all came there. "Shall I repeat it over to you?"

"Oh, yes, yes!" cried Aggie, in great glee.

"And let us have no more preliminary fibs," said George, "you are the greatest fellow for them, you know, Guy."

"Oh, p'shaw!" ejaculated Gus, impatient, "Let him go ahead!"

"That's just what the birds say," replied Guy, throwing himself back on the grass, and smiling gravely. "That big fellow on the bough there tells me he is delighted; that he has at last found one that can understand his language, for he has heard so many ridiculous theories advanced by men with picks on their shoulders and books in their hands, as to what gold is, and how it came on the ground, that he has nearly burst his throat in trying to make them understand the truth, and has then been accused of making a 'senseless chatter.'"

"And all the time," says he, "their chatter was far more senseless than mine, and so they would think if they had heard all of us laugh over their conjectures about a matter we knew all about, for birds have legends as well as men, and there's none better remembered than that of the 'Enchanted Yellow Men.'

"Thousands of years ago they inhabited the finest portions of this land. They hunted the deer on a hundred hills, and bathed in all the streams of the mountains. Their tents were in every valley, and the tracks of their feet on every path. They were the most numerous and powerful people on all the earth, yet none could tell why they were feared, for they had never battled with their neighbors, or shown great courage in the chase. In reality, it was their color alone that inspired awe. They were of the hue of the sun at midday, and their long hair streamed upon the wind like the dead leaves of corn in autumn. From toe to crown they were pure, bright yellow,—as yellow as the buttercups in yonder field.

"Ever were they looked upon with awe by their tawny brethren, who thought that the great Spirit had set the seal of his special love upon them, and had sent them forth as his chosen people. The yellow men believed the same, for everything they undertook prospered. None of the surrounding tribes ever showed opposition to them. They could follow the game over any ground, and spear the fish in any stream they chose, so that hunger never entered their wigwams; and in course of time they became so puffed up with their good fortune that they called themselves 'gods,' and the neighboring tribes bowed and worshipped them.

"Then the Great Spirit, who, from his home in the great mountains, had been watching their doings, grew very angry and threatened to destroy them all. But they were so beautiful to look upon, that he decided to try them once more and see if any good remained in them. Shortly after this a mighty tribe on the west of the yellow men, crossed over to the east, and took from a small, weak tribe that dwelt there all their lands, and drove them up to the barren mountains, where they could not find even so much as a herb to eat.

"But they were very near the Great Spirit, and he heard all their woes, and he sent a messenger down to the yellow men bidding them arise, slay the invaders and restore the destitute to their homes again. But they would not, and all those upon the mountains died, and their curses came down, and rested upon the rich and powerful who had refused to help them, and upon the day that the last of the wanderers perished a voice was heard in the tents of the yellow men, and it said, 'As ye refused to leave your lands to aid your brethren, ye shall rest in the ground till strangers shall bear thee hence, and as ye have refused to toil, or bless in your life time, ye shall do both after death. Ye shall buy food for the poor, but yet shall the curses of the Great Spirit follow ye.'

"And even as they listened to these terrible words, flames burst out of the mountains, and rushed over the valleys and and plains. As it passed over them each was burnt to a shapeless mass. In thousands of places the earth opened and they sank into their graves. And there the yellow men, in their new forms, waited for thousands of years, and there many of them are waiting still for the pick of the miner to bring them forth into their new life, to curse the wicked and improvident, and to bless the poor and needy."

"There! there! the bird has flown away!" said Aggie.

"But he has answered the question that has been puzzling my head for a long, long time," said Guy. And told us, too, that none of us should be inactive and the greater our power to help others the more we should exercise it."

"That's so," said George, "and I suppose we are all like the 'yellow men,' a good deal puffed up with our own conceit. I'll tell you what, suppose we all enter into a contract to do all the good we can, and let Guy be the judge of our actions, for after all he is the one that first put it into my head to do *any* good, you know."

"Agreed," cried Aggie, while Gus said, "It was a jolly good idea." But Guy demurred about being judge, thinking with a good deal of shame that he was sometimes as inactive in a good cause as the "yellow men" themselves.

So they sat in the woods talking the matter over until the last rays of the sun fell through the thick leaves and warned them home. Then they took their baskets and turned their faces homeward. Guy saying, "Well then, we are agreed all of us to begin the lives now, to which the "yellow men" were doomed for their idleness and presumption. Henceforth we are to help the weak, oppose the proud and wicked, and strive to do good."

"I will for one," said George, earnestly.

"So will I," echoed Gus.

"And so will I, with all my heart!" exclaimed little Aggie, just as they stepped out of the woods into the open field. "Only look," she added, glancing back, "a bird has followed us out of the woods. I do believe it is the one that told us the pretty story,—and, listen, to what he is singing, 'Good bye! why, I even can interpret that, 'Good boy! good bye! Guy Loring! Guy, Good bye!'"

[THE END.]

www.ingramcontent.com/pod-product-compliance
Lightning Source LLC
Chambersburg PA
CBHW021810230426
43669CB00008B/700